Why Enough
Is Never Enough

Why Enough
Is Never Enough

Overcoming
Worries about Money —
A Catholic Perspective

Gregory S. Jeffrey

Our Sunday Visitor Publishing Division
Our Sunday Visitor, Inc.
Huntington, Indiana 46750

Nihil Obstat
Msgr. Michael Heintz, Ph.D.
Censor Librorum

Imprimatur
✠ Kevin C. Rhoades
Bishop of Fort Wayne-South Bend
September 17, 2010

The *Nihil Obstat* and *Imprimatur* are declarations that a work is free from doctrinal or moral error. It is not implied that those who have granted the *Nihil Obstat* and *Imprimatur* agree with the contents, opinions, or statements expressed.

The Scripture citations contained in this work are taken from the *Second Catholic Edition of the Revised Standard Version of the Bible* (RSV), copyright © 1965, 1966, 2006 by the Division of Christian Education of the National Council of the Churches of Christ in the United States of America. Used by permission. All rights reserved.

Excerpts from the *Catechism of the Catholic Church, Second Edition*, for use in the United States of America, copyright © 1994 and 1997, United States Catholic Conference — Libreria Editrice Vaticana. Used by permission. All rights reserved.

Every reasonable effort has been made to determine copyright holders of excerpted materials and to secure permissions as needed. If any copyrighted materials have been inadvertently used in this work without proper credit being given in one form or another, please notify Our Sunday Visitor in writing so that future printings of this work may be corrected accordingly.

ISBN 978-1-59276-743-4 (Inventory No. T1064)
LCCN: 2010936167

Interior design by M. Urgo
Cover design by Rebecca J. Heaston
Cover photo by Shutterstock

PRINTED IN THE UNITED STATES OF AMERICA

*To my parents — my first teachers —
and the Sisters of St. Benedict,
who by their lives taught me
what it means to be generous.*

Contents

Chapter 1

How Much Is Enough?

Even now, twenty years later, the thing that strikes me most about the attack is how abruptly it both began and ended. I was leaning on a barricade, watching for a friend to come up the escalator at the Brixton Underground in London's East End, when a punch from behind sent my glasses flying. The blow spun me around, and within seconds the assailant landed several more, bloodying my nose and breaking bones in my left hand. "What did I do?" I yelled, stupidly assuming that senseless violence needed a reason. There was none. Apparently, this is why it's called "senseless violence."

But I must have said the right thing. Within seconds, he was gone. No words. No demands. No money. He left as quickly as he had come.

The entrance foyer, bustling with scores of evening commuters less than a minute ago, was now empty. The newspaper and flower vendors instinctively lowered the metal grates protecting their stalls, and I was left alone, shaking uncontrollably, and wondering what had just happened.

I begin with this story not to engender sympathy, but in an admittedly odd way, to give you hope. I recently moved from North Dakota to Washington, D.C., and memories of that day follow me every time I board the subway. But as I nervously scan the faces of my fellow commuters, I realize that fear of attack is worse than the thing itself. The beating hurt, but it really wasn't that bad. It lasted only about thirty seconds. Fear, on the other hand, has proven more detrimental because it's a daily companion. To live on the defense is no way to live.

In like fashion, many of us spend our entire lives worrying about money — about what would happen if we lost our job or our home — or wondering if we'll be able to retire with any degree of comfort. Financially, we live life on the defense. Moral of the story: I believe worries about personal financial collapse are more crippling than the actual event, if indeed adversity ever strikes. And knowing this should, in a roundabout way, give us hope. As my father used to say, "Worrying is just something to do until the real thing happens."

There is an unstated assumption that money brings freedom and a sense of liberty. To some extent that's true. People are correct when they speak of the "chains of poverty." To be hungry and homeless leaves room for little else in the day other than thoughts of food and shelter.

Even in less extreme cases, the hardship caused by temporary unemployment is equally real. I recall economics classes in business school that outlined the social and interpersonal damage of recession: stress, family strife, divorce, bitterness, fear, and delayed health care and education. It is particularly hard on marriage, and since the future of society is built on today's family, poverty and unemployment have extensive consequences, especially when it affects parents' relationship with each other.

But this gray haze of financial worry is not limited to the poor. It seems to be spreading throughout the

American psyche. Even those with good jobs, savings, and an upper-middle-class lifestyle are not immune, especially when the economy limps through recession. Persistent worries about money are a weight that millions live with every day, sapping the joy of life.

This is not how our Creator intended us to live. It burdens me greatly to see so many people anxious about money, scrambling to attain an illusive security that's never quite achieved. The question, then, is where do we start? How do we find peace in the midst of economic worry?

The first step is to realize that more money — the assumed sole solution to the problem — actually plays a relatively small part in curing persistent financial anxiety. In fact, as wealth increases, it actually becomes an illusion with its own set of worries. Admittedly, this is completely counterintuitive, but a thought experiment might help.

Imagine a young child growing up poor. His parents do their best to provide, but he is often hungry and the family moves frequently as his father searches for work. Anxieties about employment and money are constant companions.

Then as a young adult he discovers his talent as a salesman. By the age of twenty-seven, he is the top performer at a large company. Our young businessman can finally afford a deluxe apartment, and he no longer remembers what it feels like to be hungry.

By the age of thirty-two, he has saved up enough money to buy his first home. Later, a confident business presentation produces the loan he needs to start his own company. Tasting success, he consistently works sixty hours per week. By the time he's forty-five, his annual take-home pay is well over $300,000. He buys a bigger house and the $45,000 car he always wanted.

Life is good, evidenced by his waistline. The poverty of his youth used to keep it in check, but the external restraint forced by lack of money must now be replaced with internal discipline — an irony he hadn't foreseen. So much for eat, drink, and be merry.

Then one morning at age fifty-five, he looks in the mirror and notices, as if for the first time, his receding gray hair. Where have the years gone? What he sees is a stark reminder that retirement is nearing. So he spends more time with investment advisors, and at least an hour each day reading the financial news and checking on stocks. His primary concern shifts from making money to protecting and investing the assets he's worked so hard to acquire, a time-consuming endeavor on top of an already overextended work schedule.

But a lifetime of effort pays off handsomely. By age sixty-five our friend has attained the American Dream. As he makes final preparations for retirement, a team of accountants offers advice on the business and tax consequences of several decisions when a startling thought occurs to him: *I can't possibly consume everything I've acquired.*

This scenario illustrates my first general premise: Poverty is real. But wealth is an illusion. As income increases, we eventually reach a point of satiation. One can only eat so much before health begins to falter. One can only purchase a certain amount of possessions before running out of room to store them. And even if a larger home is purchased — preferably with a three-car garage and walk-in closets — how long before this home, too, is cluttered with flotsam and jetsam? At some point an individual can only consume so much. Then the concern shifts from satisfying needs and wants to protecting the wealth already acquired. *From this point onward wealth becomes increasingly illusory.*

Granted, the point of satiation differs between people. For some families, a salary of $100,000 might be more than they ever dreamed of earning and more than enough to meet every need and want. For others it might be two or three times that much. Still others might spend $1 million to satisfy their material desires.

I'm making no judgment here on those fond of material possessions. I'm merely stating an obvious fact that many fail to notice: each of us has a point at which added income does not translate into added consumption or pleasure. Somewhere along the continuum each of us has a point at which we satisfy our immediate desires. From that point forward additional money burdens us with a question: what will we do with it?

I can hear the reader's challenge, "Try me! I would love to know what it feels like to be 'burdened' with more money than I can spend!" Fine. Let's go down that path.

You may be tempted to think that if you just had "X" more in your paycheck, you would easily find a way to spend it on yourself or your family. I'm sure this is true for the vast majority of Americans. So imagine yourself with 10 percent added to your paycheck. It's easy to envision ways to spend an extra 10 percent. Now keep going. What would you do with twice the income? What if you earned ten, or one hundred or a thousand times your current income? Imagine winning the Powerball lottery and going from $40,000 a year to $40 million overnight. How would you possibly spend $40 million on yourself and your family? You wouldn't. Everything beyond the first few million would very likely go unused, which makes me wonder why so many more people flock to state lotteries when the jackpot tops $100 million and the odds of winning fall to near zero. Whether it's $20 million or $100 million, what real difference does it make to the winner? It's impossible to use it all. The extra cash is just a number, photo op, and bragging rights.

This mental exercise illustrates a principle: as income increases, money no longer means a full stomach or shelter or clothing, but a number on a bank statement. Whether increasing a paycheck by 10 percent or a thousand fold, each individual reaches his or her own unique point where there is no desire to purchase any more "stuff." Needs and wants are satisfied, for now, and well into the future. Additional income simply becomes a time-consuming concern — what shall I do with it? At *precisely* this point more wealth becomes increasingly meaningless.

This is a difficult concept to comprehend because we hold an assumption that more wealth is *always* better, that it always brings greater security. In reality, it is true that wealth initially creates an envelope of security. This is the part of the journey that most understand, because the rise from adolescence to middle age entails, for the majority, a struggle up this curve. Having experienced the security that *some* wealth brings, there is an assumption that more wealth brings even more security. Thus the notion, soon to be proven false, that "financial freedom" is ultimately found when one has enough wealth.

In fact, research suggests that beyond $20,000, added income actually has little direct impact on self-reported levels of happiness. Michael Shermer, professor of economics at Claremont Graduate University, summarizes research that suggests money influences happiness at a much lower point than most of us would likely guess:

> Arguably the most penetrating and most international study of happiness ever conducted is that of the World Values Survey that includes 250 questions that yield four hundred to eight hundred measurable variables. Over the past thirty years the survey shows that while people in certain pockets of the globe experience temporary increases or decreases in happiness, the average level of happiness has remained essentially unchanged. Once average income is above $20,000 per annum in today's dollars — enough to put a roof over your head and provide three square meals a day for you and your family — more money does not bring more happiness.[1]

Richard Easterlin, professor of economics at the University of Southern California, examined economic data for Japan from 1962 to 1987, coupled with social science data on self-reported happiness. In a postwar era that saw Japan's per-capita Gross Domestic Product increase 3.5-fold, "Happiness remained constant despite Japan's remarkable economic growth."[2]

Yet many Americans still relentlessly strive for wealth, without pausing to ponder this phenomenon: when needs and desires are satisfied, everything beyond that is "stored" in the event that we may need it later. But whether one dies with $10,000,000 in the bank or a mere $1,000, what difference does it make? It may make a great deal of difference to Uncle Sam and your heirs, but what difference does it make to *you*? You're dead. If you leave behind $10 million, all it means is that you made a horrible miscalculation as to the amount of money you needed.

I'm being a bit harsh. Certainly, every parent wants his or her children to do well, and I can understand the comfort of dying with the knowledge that loved ones will be cared for financially. But at what cost? Even if you never attain great wealth, realize it is not only illusory but *deceptive* — even in the modest doses that signal entry to the middle class — because wealth is thrice time-consuming: to earn it, spend it, and invest it. By its nature wealth is about the acquisition and disposition of *things*. Every hour spent in this endeavor is one less hour spent in *relationship*.

I had a professor in business school who used to say, "You either have time or money; you rarely have both." To see an illustration of this principle, we need look no further than the front porch of our homes. My first house in Winona, Minnesota, was in a very old section of town, with neighbors of modest means. On most summer evenings half the porches were filled with people enjoying the evening air. The view is humble, but on Winona's porches you will still find husbands and wives sitting together after dinner, watching their children play ball or ride bicycles up and down the sidewalk. It's a scene repeated throughout small-town America.

Contrast this with the upscale high-rise apartments in our cities. It's a much better view from these balconies, so why are they empty? Where are the people? Most likely they are at the office working late — so they can afford a view they are too busy to enjoy.

Automobiles are another good example of the trade-off between material goods and relationships. I've known people who drove expensive cars, but I've never understood the attraction. It wasn't just the cost of upkeep that I found objectionable. These cars also consumed time and a certain amount of emotional energy. Owners only trusted certain mechanics. The car had to be kept spotless. Like a mother protecting a newborn, they were reluctant to park anywhere a door ding might be possible, and if the slightest scratch were to appear, it was like a death in the family. Sadly, they did not see the emotional investment they were making in a *thing* rather than a *person*.

On the other hand, I have a brother-in-law who lives on the edge of an Indian reservation in the Minnesota north woods. One day the tribal elders paid him a visit with a complaint: parking his car in public view was apparently bringing down property values.

Admittedly, the car was ready for the iron smelter. But it didn't matter to him. Instead, his interest was focused on six happy, fun-loving children who got his best time and attention. Here is a man who understands a very important trade-off: we can spend our time keeping up *things* or keeping up *relationships*. Wealth invites us, ever so slowly and with great cunning, to spend more time on things rather than people. Wealth is deceptive.

This shift from people to things is never dramatic. If it were, most of us would catch ourselves short and resist the temptation. Rather, wealth warms up to us slowly. With no little irony, I have come to envision wealth as a beggar. The opening gambit never raises alarm: "Excuse me, buddy, do you have a minute?" From there it escalates. The "minute" spent with matters of wealth — earning, spending, investing — turns into hours that soon become days.

I'm not immune from this phenomenon. Last year was a financially successful one for me, and as December approached I began to wonder whether I should invest in a new computer. Despite what I told my wife, I didn't really need one. I could have gotten by with my two-year-old notebook. But I was tempted, so I began looking for a reason to justify the decision. After an evening spent reviewing business records, I decided that I could really use the tax deduction. Having happily found an excuse to proceed, I spent hours on Web research and visits to the big-box stores.

A week later UPS delivered a custom-built machine that sat in its packing material for two months because I was too busy to bother with the setup and software installations, an anticipated six-hour endeavor. When I finally transferred my software and files to the new computer, I discovered a hardware problem that required factory service and a trip to UPS. Bottom line: the new computer — one I honestly didn't need — required perhaps twenty hours of my life, including a beautiful spring Sunday and several evenings. Instead of focusing on a machine, I could have spent that time with my wife, or phoning family members, or visiting relatives in the nursing home. I spent time on a *thing* instead of *relationships*. That computer is just *one* item. Americans make millions of purchases every year. Extrapolate from this example, and it becomes apparent how wealth seduces a nation, sapping time from relationships and devoting it instead to things.

Having said all this, I am not antimaterialistic. It's good to have a pleasant home and possessions that delight our senses. The same is true for savings and investments. It's wise to save money for a rainy day to provide some security and insurance against life's inevitable challenges. I'm merely illustrating two characteristics of wealth — its illusory and deceptive qualities — that many experience but rarely acknowledge. As you read, keep these two points in mind because they inform every corollary in the following chapters and set the stage for financial freedom that is real and lasting.

Now let's turn to the central question of this chapter: "At what point can I quit worrying about money?"

Before going further, I need to clarify the question. I'm not referring to an immediate or short-term cash-crunch that most of us inevitably experience. If you need $800 for rent by Thursday, you can quit worrying about money when you have $800! That's pretty obvious. The question I'm trying to answer concerns the overarching financial anxiety that so many people live with on a daily basis, even those with good jobs and some savings.

In this case, how much money is required for a person to finally feel secure?

The short answer: that number does not exist. Financial anxiety is not *necessarily* a function of having or not having money.

I've worked as a professional fund-raiser since 1986, and in that time I've had the privilege of visiting in-person with more than 3,500 individuals across the nation to ask their support of various causes, from education to construction projects for parishes. With such a wide sample it was inevitable that I would meet the ultrawealthy as well as those of significantly more modest means. In many instances well-dressed executives pledged hundreds of thousands to their alma mater. In another case, I fondly remember a farm family offering a truckload of grain to support their parish project, plus a dozen free-range eggs as a tip for making the trip to see them.

Reflecting on my career and those thousands of visits, I discovered an interesting phenomenon. More than a few poor people never really worry about money. Conversely, I've met wealthy individuals that worried constantly. This is counterintuitive. Apparently, to feel a sense of financial freedom, something is at play other than the amount of money in one's savings and investments. Put another way, *financial freedom is not the same thing as having money.*

This is antithetical to current thinking. There are thousands of books and articles promising "financial freedom" with the unstated assumption that if one had enough money, worries, at least in the financial realm, would cease. This assumption is not necessarily true.

First, define "enough." This alone is an impossible task. I recall my first assignment as a fund-raising consultant with a major national firm. Despite the Notre Dame pedigree, I was still very much a small town kid. I grew up in East Grand Forks, Minnesota, on the border with Grand Forks, North Dakota. Farming has long been the mainstay of the local economy, and it imprints upon the people an outlook on life that others might find peculiar: in an agrarian culture, it's not polite to be wealthy. More precisely, there were people I knew who likely *had* wealth, but God forbid that one should *appear* wealthy. Driving a new truck every two years bordered on acceptable, but purchasing a full-length fur for "The Mrs." would require quite a bit of explaining, as in, "The doctor said it was the only thing that would protect her arthritic knees from the minus-30 degree wind-chill...."

So I was not accustomed to the trappings of wealth. Still, as part of my first assignment I helped orchestrate a fund-raising function on a 110-foot yacht. The idea was to sail Milwaukee's harbor for an evening, providing an opportunity for the charity's top administrators to get to know those kind enough to join us.

The yacht required a crew of three, and as guests boarded, we were asked to remove our shoes. Thankful for the foresight to wear new socks, I soon learned why we were asked to enjoy a near-barefoot cruise: the entire interior of the ship was decked out in plush white carpet. It was quite striking. More accustomed to my father's sixteen-foot bass boat, I tried hard to keep from gushing. With cool reserve, I managed a suitable comment to the wife of the captain: "You have a lovely yacht."

She graciously responded, "*We* like it." Little did I know at the time that "We like it" is standard protocol for the wealthy, but you have to say it right: matter-of-factly with an emphasis on "*we*." I've since heard the same response beautifully delivered scores of times. Recited well, it gives the impression that the article currently admired is really no big deal. And to the captain's wife, perhaps it wasn't. Here we discover, in this small comment, a sidebar truth about wealth: After thousands of major gift solicitation calls, I have yet to meet anyone who saw himself as wealthy. Perhaps it's because wealth is relative, and unless you are Bill Gates or Warren Buffett, there will always be someone else who apparently has more.

So how much is "enough"? At what point does one quit worrying about money? Again, worry doesn't necessarily diminish as one's assets grow. I recall a gentleman who verbally committed $100,000 to a charity, but sternly cautioned that if his wife found out, we wouldn't get a dime, presumably because she would take it — along with everything else — in a divorce. He went on to admit that even if he were to lose his job, his family would be secure. With melancholy and exasperation, he said, "My wife doesn't understand that we have enough money to last several lifetimes." Despite this knowledge, his spouse worried incessantly.

This is not a lone instance of a particular neurosis. In my experience as a solicitor, it is actually not uncommon. People across the socioeconomic spectrum assume that if they just made more, they would finally feel a sense of financial freedom.[3] Not so.

Thus, my general premise: enough is never enough. There is a certain amount of money that will fill your belly, shelter your family, educate your children, and see you through retirement. But there is no amount of money that can necessarily give you real and lasting financial freedom. For that you must make peace with money.

That's what this book is about: making personal peace with money. I will show you how to do that. Not how to *make money*, but how to *make peace* with money. And God.

FOR REFLECTION

One of the purposes of this book is to help you overcome persistent anxieties about money. That's why each chapter concludes with an exercise to help you reflect on the topic just discussed.

These exercises will be more helpful if you work through them with a close friend. As you will see in the next chapter, we need others to keep us honest with ourselves. So as a first step you are encouraged to invite a friend, your spouse, or other trusted individual to work through this book and these exercises with you.

Who would you like to invite to be your "money partner"? List the names of three people with whom you would be comfortable discussing money.

Once you've found a money partner, answer the following questions in preparation for a discussion with him or her. If that's not possible, proceed on your own with a promise to yourself to give serious thought to these questions:

Wealth Is Illusory

1. Assuming you received a 10 percent raise today, what would you do with the extra money?

2. Assuming you tripled your income, what would you change about your life? What would you do with the added money?

3. How much would you need to make to satisfy *all* your needs and wants? What is that number? Take some time to think about this. Be honest. If it's a big number, that's okay, as long as you are honest with yourself.

4. Now, triple *that* number again. On a practical level, how would your daily life change? Would it change? What would the extra money do for you?

Wealth Is Deceptive

This chapter offered the example of an unneeded notebook computer to illustrate how possessions can shift our attention from people to things.

1. Do you have any possessions that demand your time?

2. Can you think of any circumstances in your own life similar to the example offered in this chapter?

Chapter 2

Making Peace with Money

Children are taught there are certain things not discussed in polite conversation: politics, religion, sex, and money. There may be wisdom in this counsel. Casual conversation, the kind we make with acquaintances instead of friends, is better suited to topics not quite so close to the heart.

For example, I recently acquired a new barber near Dupont Circle in Washington, D.C. With the change in the administration I half-jokingly asked who were better tippers, Republicans or Democrats. My stylist promptly responded, "I don't discuss politics." Smart man.

Yet, despite better judgment, the conversation eventually drifted back toward the election. I should have taken my parents' advice and avoided talking politics: as I thanked him and walked out the door I felt disappointed, even a bit melancholy.

I wondered if he felt the same. In the course of an hour together, we each tentatively shared a few thoughts about public policy, and quickly sensed that if the conversation went much further we would discover we were on opposite sides of most issues — an uncomfortable position neither of us wanted to be in. But that's not the frustrating part. The disappointment comes in feeling I had knowledge and experience that could have broadened his viewpoint. I trust he felt this too; I might have learned a thing or two from him.

Instead the conversation stopped short. I instinctively knew that if politics are to be discussed on a meaningful level, an individual must eventually share the life experiences that shape attitudes. For my stylist, that would mean entrusting to me his painful stories of growing up gay in a small Midwest town, a bit of history he only hinted at, and I would eventually need to admit how God used my own arrogance to humble me. These are the real experiences that shape our view of the world, our attitudes, and ultimately our politics. But sharing these sorts of life experiences, by definition, requires one person to enter into a relationship with the other person. Since this would not be possible with just thirty minutes in the barber chair once a month, we had a polite conversation that dabbled in politics, but avoided the kind of personal discussion that could have been of great profit to both. Sadly, it was another of those missed opportunities to be human.

This phenomenon is widespread in our culture. Although politics has become a staple of American conversation, it is rarely discussed with an intimacy that reveals our deeper motivations. Instead we talk past each other, superficially arguing policy and position, reticent to allow another to probe the experiences and wounds that animate our opinions and beliefs. We're reluctant to share on a personal, human level. Conversation of this kind would force us to reveal ourselves, wounds and all. This, in turn, would invite self-examination, and, frankly, we may not like what we find.

Thus, in politics and other matters close to the heart, there is a natural tendency to keep the focus of discussion outward and intellectual. We resist self-reflection. This resistance applies most poignantly to the topic of money. Ironically, Americans talk about money all the time, but in a superficial way that only discusses how to make it and keep it. Enter any men's locker room after work. The air is full of talk about business and money: who's making it, losing it, borrowing it, bathing in it. Yet we are reluctant to talk about money at that place where wealth intersects with the soul.

What does this say about money? I contend that in modern life it has become as intimate to our person as politics, religion, or even sex. I've had more than one heart-to-heart talk about my love life with friends, or even a trusted sister-in-law, but have never discussed money with the same degree of intimacy. Sure, I've talked about life insurance, the stock market, and the economy on many occasions. But I don't recall ever having a heart-to-heart talk about money at that place where greed and generosity, fear and courage, do battle. That is private turf.

Perhaps this rings true in your life, too. *Little wonder few of us are at peace with money.* On this topic we rarely if ever benefit from the therapy of an in-depth exchange of hearts.

This is unfortunate. Without the reflective mirror that others provide, we have a painfully difficult time acknowledging and understanding our own attitudes and behaviors, including those concerning money.

Again, Americans talk about money all the time. But casual talk about business and investing is not the same as examining our soul's relationship with money. Few people "go there." Few examine why they hold certain attitudes or adopt certain behaviors. For example, what motivates a spendthrift? Why are others notoriously frugal? Some people immediately feel guilty and annoyed when asked to support a charity; others cringe at the thought of asking friends to support a cause. Why? What lies behind our attitude toward money?

Experience early in life certainly accounts for part of an explanation. Those who went through the Great Depression as children often have very conservative attitudes about money. This is understandable on a psychological level. But our interest here is deeper. To make peace with money, one's relationship with money must be examined on a *spiritual* level. That requires grace, humility, self-assessment, and an honest friend willing to help us see ourselves as we really are.

Herein lies the blessing of spending one's life asking for alms. I've had these talks with thousands of people, because it's impossible to raise money without talking about money, one-on-one, in a very intimate way. Thus my career has given me a vantage point from which to understand one of man's deepest and most intimate connections: our bond with money.[4]

In 1991, Tom Suddes was kind enough to give me — with a newly-minted MBA — a job despite his outspoken disdain for those with the degree. At the risk of paraphrasing another, he felt an advanced business degree created eggheads who were paid to dream up schemes that attempted to defy the laws of financial physics. Given the recent economic collapse, he may have been right.

Tom served the University of Notre Dame as a development officer, then went on to found a consulting group that applied the Notre Dame model of fund-raising to Catholic secondary education. He hired consultants well seasoned at the nation's best universities, and as a young man I was fortunate to learn from the group's collective experience.

In an effort to continually improve our service, we gathered once a month for two days. Tom, trained as a paratrooper, privately referred to his crew at these gatherings as "Marines out of uniform." Despite the military overtones in language and style, the meetings could best be described as stream-of-consciousness, which in an odd way actually made them quite productive. My colleagues freely talked about concerns most pressing to them; in those days that translated into issues most pressing to our clients. Every conversation eventually turned back to our central task as consultants: getting appointments on behalf of our clients and asking individuals for gifts larger than they cared to consider.

I recall our first company meeting. Someone brought up for review the solicitations they had done earlier in the week and remarked how, when asking for money, "The room turns into a confessional."

Though I didn't understand at the time, I have come to appreciate the profundity of this analogy. For those not familiar with the Sacrament of Reconciliation, or "Confession" in popular parlance, it is the one place where an individual can courageously face his sinfulness and unburden himself of guilt. That's quite a gift. Approached with unbridled honesty, it's therapeutic; paired with humility, it has the power to rescue us from ourselves.

When asking people for money, the room often does "turn into a confessional." I've seen it enough over the years to sense it while it is still on the horizon, like smelling salt air before catching the first glimpse of the sea. These are the conversations that go beyond, "I'd love to help but, frankly, my company is not doing well." That's an admission, not a confession.

No, discussion of money or business is only the starting point. From there the conversation leads to every imaginable facet of people's lives. This is where the "confession" begins. I go into an executive's office to ask for support of a charity, and next thing I know we're talking about his marital troubles, an estranged son, or a daughter's cancer. I'm told of hurtful comments made decades ago, of wrongs never righted, and decisions that would be made differently if given a chance. It's amazing how so many facets of life are touched by money. As the hour concludes, I often come away feeling I was privy to a part of their interior life rarely examined, and almost never revealed.

Maybe I've just been graced with the unthreatening face of a beagle, allowing people to get things off their chest. I don't think so. Others in the profession, as noted above, speak of the same experience. This leads to my central hypothesis: *perhaps we sidestep intimate conversations about money precisely because it leads to other sensitive areas of life, some in need of profound healing.* We avoid the "confessional." Unfortunately, this leaves us hidden from ourselves, with our deepest feelings about money unexamined. If my hypothesis is correct, it's easy to understand why so few are at peace with money, even those who have wealth.

This brings us to the central question of this chapter, as yet unanswered: *What does it mean to be at peace with money?*

After twenty-plus years of solicitation, I can usually tell when someone has found this peace, sometimes even in the initial conversation. Even so, it's still devilishly difficult to explain. It's like trying to define love, which is readily apparent when we experience it, yet impossible to adequately describe. St. Paul made perhaps the best attempt to explain love in his first letter to the Corinthians. But even with divine inspiration, the best he could do was say, "Love is patient and kind" (1 Cor 13:4). Then he went on to define love by describing what love does *not* do. He lists the *behaviors* that are *absent* when one is acting out of love. "Love is not jealous or boastful; it is not arrogant or rude. Love does not insist on its own way; it is not irritable or resentful; it does not rejoice at wrong, but rejoices in the right" (1 Cor 13:4–6).

In a roundabout way, St. Paul's way of defining love offers us a method to explain what it means to be at peace with money. We can say a little about the characteristics of someone who has found peace and then go on to describe at length the *behaviors* of someone who is *not at peace*.

There are two characteristics I see in those who have made peace with money. First, there is a belief that things will be all right, even in dire circumstances. Periodic worry, which is a natural part of the economic life of man, is overshadowed by faith that one's basic needs will be met. Second, this underlying faith animates a spirit of generosity that pervades every aspect of life. Later, we'll explore the spiritual aspects of the virtue of generosity. For now, suffice it to say this attribute is the same virtue we teach children in kindergarten: Share your toys. Give half your candy bar to your brother. Take turns.

These two attributes, faith and generosity, are well developed in the person at peace with money, but they are sometimes hard to see. Like St. Paul trying to describe what love does *not* do, it's easier to describe typical behaviors of someone *not* at peace with money.

Let us turn, then, to self examination. Do you see yourself in any of the following seven scenarios?

1. *The person who has not made peace with money often suffers from a pervasive anxiety about their finances.*

As I discussed in the first chapter, I'm not talking about specific worries concerning specific obligations. That's understandable. Rather, I am referring to an overarching unease about money that never lifts. This type of anxiety is independent of one's financial status; even the wealthy are not immune. You may rightly wonder how the poor, those who literally live paycheck-to-paycheck or worse, could ever escape such anxiety but, paradoxically, many do. I need look no further than my own childhood, to my parents and aunts and uncles, to know such a thing is possible.

My mother was the fourth of eighteen children. While they were fortunate to be able to raise their own meat, keep hens for eggs, and grow garden vegetables, their farmhouse in northwest Minnesota had no running water, no plumbing, and a wood stove for heat and cooking. It was the early 1970s before my grandmother, already past retirement age, finally moved to a home with indoor plumbing.

As a young child we would visit my grandparents. Given the vagaries of Minnesota weather, we would see them more often in the summer. I still recall the unscreened windows wide open, and a cool breeze that never quite compensated for the heavy smell of the wood stove. My mother sometimes sat me on Grandpa's lap, which required a bit of courage on my part. Grandpa was a good man, but I was very shy, and his well-worn face, missing teeth, and scent of snuff and an honest day's work left me counting the minutes until mother returned. Above all, he rarely, if ever, spoke English, and I didn't speak Polish. So to pass the time, I would look out the window at the chickens roaming the yard. When that curiosity was satisfied, I would sit quietly and marvel at the flypaper hung strategically over the wood stove, wondering if the flies ever worked themselves free, only to fall wingless to their deaths in the soup kettle below. Looking back, I find it amazing how children find ways to entertain themselves.

Parents back then and "out there" were equally good at keeping children busy. We lived in a small town, just a few blocks from the fields. After the potato harvest each fall, my mother would give my older brother and me two paper bags and send us out to the field to glean the baby red potatoes left behind by the machines. Maybe she just wanted to get us out of her hair for a couple of hours. Maybe she really needed the potatoes. All I know is that my brother and I would proudly waddle home, each carrying a bag of baby reds, and Mom would greet us with an approving smile.

In hindsight, the potatoes were probably part of the family budget. My mom had an eighth-grade education, and my father, for various reasons, slightly less. Mom stayed at home and Dad worked long hours for very little money. When they were paying bills I often heard Mom reassure Dad, "Oh, we'll make it." Even in retirement she still says that, except now I know what it means for a family: we found a way to stretch the paycheck through yet another month.

Despite the circumstances, I never sensed in my parents a debilitating anxiety about money. If it did exist, certainly I would have noticed. Children know everything. Even when my father lost his job at the potato chip factory, I never heard arguing or accusations. Instead, Dad took a longer-than-usual nap after dinner, while Mom quietly broke the news to us.

In short, there is no doubt that my parents were among the millions of families that literally lived paycheck-to-paycheck. But because they were at peace with money, there was no pervasive anxiety burdening the family.

2. *The person who has not made peace with money has a predisposition to compare his or her financial status with others.*

I recently watched a documentary featuring a Brazilian aboriginal tribe that lived deep in the Amazon rain forest. Day after day they ate nothing but fish and a root harvested from the jungle. It was a subsistence life with none of the amenities of modernity. Yet the reporter remarked, "I've never seen such happy people." The video told the same story: laughter pervaded their day.

How can this be explained? How is it possible to be so happy with so little?

One explanation is maybe they just didn't know any better. It's impossible to miss cars, cell phones, electricity, modern dental care, and microwave-ready food if you don't know they exist. One has to wonder what would happen if members of that Brazilian tribe were to see others with certain amenities. Would they grow to desire them as well? Would they complain about the unequal global distribution of Chicken McNuggets, or would they remain content with fish and roots?

Unlike our aboriginal friends, Americans are rarely satisfied. This stems from a predisposition to compare one's financial status with others. Simply put, the person who has not made peace with money suffers from a concern that somebody else is making more. I'm not referring to a sense of justice that underpins equal pay for equal work. Rather, I'm talking about an instinctive inclination to compare one's success not with regard *to what one is called to do*, but rather in relation to the financial success of one's peers. This is certain to needlessly unsettle the soul, but it's painfully common.

There was a fascinating study done recently in which people were asked which they would prefer: earn $50,000 while others were earning $25,000, or earn $100,000 while others were earning $250,000. The report notes: "Surprisingly — stunningly, in fact — research shows that the majority of people select the first option:

they would rather make twice as much as others even if that meant earning half as much as they could have."[5]

This is an extremely telling study about our culture. The results speak directly to the issue of jealousy and its close cousin, envy. Sadly, these self-chosen attitudes sap as much joy from people's lives as material poverty, which makes me wonder why people affectionately cling to them. It's one thing to worry about meeting the material needs of life; I can understand stress that emanates from an empty stomach. It's quite another thing, however, to worry that someone else has *more* than you. This type of worry is the most senseless of anxieties, and it's a classic symptom of someone who has yet to make peace with money.

3. The person who has not made peace with money has an unwillingness to recognize his or her own good fortune.

At face value, this is an odd symptom. Why wouldn't an individual want to acknowledge personal financial success? Surprisingly, it's not uncommon.

I had a business associate who was taken aback when I told him an income of $160,000 a year put him in the top 5 percent of American wage earners.[6] He looked startled. "You have to be kidding!" He also appeared annoyed, which caught me off guard. I had assumed his learning he was "playing with the big dogs" would give him a sense of pride in accomplishment but he was genuinely irritated and unsettled by the statistic. Why?

He likely was familiar with the Scripture admonition, "Every one to whom much is given, of him will much be required" (Lk 12:48). It doesn't take a rocket scientist to see where this was heading. Within seconds of learning he was in the top 5 percent of wage earners, his conscience responded with a quiet, instinctive question: "What are you going to do with it?"

I could sense that he immediately felt an interior weight. To be clear, it was not guilt, just a burden. Guilt requires knowledge. From his response, he was genuinely surprised to find he was among select company who had the wherewithal to do great things with their almsgiving. So he should have felt no guilt — he hadn't realized he was among those "to whom much is given."

But now he *knew*; God whispered to him through a simple statistic. If he didn't respond, chances were good that the burden would grow into a sense of guilt. No wonder he was annoyed. This was one of those things we feel in our bones, but don't want to face. We instinctively know that success, even success earned through one's own sacrifice and persistence, comes with certain obligations. Whether or not you're religious, natural law has written this truth on the human heart. That's why, upon learning they are in the top echelons of income, people receive the news with equal parts pride and annoyance. Little wonder my colleague preferred ignorance.

I can't say I blame him.

A few years ago my older brother decided his son was old enough for a mission trip to Haiti. They decided to go together and suggested I come along.

I refused, explaining that the people of Haiti would be much better off if I took the cost of the trip and just cut them a check. As one would expect of a well-trained lawyer, my brother persisted. No matter what I said, he countered every one of my objections. Finally he pulled out the big guns.

"This will be a *life-changing* trip," he passionately promised.

I responded with confidence. "Then I'm not going for sure."

"Why not?"

"Because I like my life just the way it is. Why would I want to change it?"

It feels good to finally stump your older brother. But it only lasted a day or so. I soon had to silently admit that I was trying to avoid the reality of my own good fortune. It's one thing to read statistics about wealth distribution in the world; it's another to experience it firsthand. I would have none of it, for a very simple reason: I didn't want to find myself called to even greater acts of generosity. Worse yet, I tried to buy my way out of the situation: thus my first gambit to skip the airfare and give him the money to buy his new friends a goat. Sadly, even almsgiving can have motivations that render an act of generosity devoid of merit. I was willing to give a *little* to avoid giving *more*.

4. The person who has not made peace with money displays greed.

A word of caution is in order. There is a tendency today to loosely use the term greed and accuse anyone with wealth of being greedy. In reality, we do a disservice to routinely link greed and wealth. Greed is a disposition of the soul, not a matter of the pocketbook. As you will see in the next chapter, even the poor can be greedy.

This may seem counterintuitive, but greed cannot be presumed by judging another's material possessions. It is a much more sophisticated illness to detect, because it is linked not to possessions, but to interior motivations. For this reason, I am reluctant to describe anyone as greedy. To pronounce judgment on another person's intentions is to walk on thin ice.

Yet the term is often used because people erroneously equate wealth with greed; the assumption is that the two must go hand-in-hand. Not necessarily. Again, wealth has to do with one's physical possessions; greed is an interior disposition, an inordinate desire. While it's important to acknowledge that greed exists, it would be a mistake to immediately assume greed is always the motivation behind the desire to grow a successful business. There can be many reasons an individual works to expand a company, and personal monetary reward is only one possible explanation.

During my first year in business school an entrepreneur gave a presentation concerning his latest endeavor, turning around a failing trucking company. He had been very successful in an unrelated industry, sold his company, and then used the proceeds to buy the trucking firm. After the presentation I asked him why he didn't just retire to a beach somewhere. He certainly had enough money to do so, which he readily acknowledged. "I guess I just enjoy the challenge of making things work," he explained to me.

I have since found this attribute among many wealthy business personalities. For this gentleman, it wasn't about the money. He just wanted another opportunity to build something for the joy of creating.

Sadly, it has become fashionable to vilify anyone who is successful, to paint all with a broad brush. For example, when is the last time Hollywood cast the rich as a champion of society? When are they portrayed as a provider of goods and services, an employer feeding families, a patron of charities and the poor? Doesn't happen. Doesn't fit the stereotype. Rather, the typical script cynically assumes that success is always motivated by, and the result of, greed.

How many of us who hold this view would see it within ourselves as a prejudice? It's no less ugly than prejudice against skin color or creed. And like all prejudice, it reveals more about the person who subscribes to it than the group being disparaged. To believe that every success is motivated by a heart filled with greed is to expose the envy in your own.

5. The person who has not made peace with money has an inability to conceive of something other than money motivating job performance and life's decisions.

This trait appears to be on the decline, perhaps due in part to the careerism of the last twenty or thirty years. Still, members of each new generation have to discover for themselves those things of lasting worth. My generation is no different.

Back in the early 1980s I had a musician friend who spent a couple of rigorous weekends earning his Series 7 license, one of the exams required by brokerage firms for their registered representatives. I'm sure the test is a challenge today, but back then it seemed a lot of my musician friends were getting certified in a very short period of time. One minute the self-proclaimed "Italian Stallion" was a guitarist looking for a gig, and the next he was a financial planner. I always envisioned stockbrokers in suits and ties. The Stallion wore a striped shirt with the top three buttons undone, along with a gold chain marking a crisp border between 'shave' and 'don't shave' zones peeking from beneath his collar.

He was a dangerously good salesman. There was something about the way he advised "Buy, diversify, and hold!" that told the client he had earned his license with the appropriate degree of fortitude. Now he was ready to expand. And where does a guitarist-turned-financial-planner turn for his first trustworthy hire? His bass player, of course.

On several occasions, usually over drinks, The Stallion urged me to work for him. The pitch was always the same. I can still see him taking a drag on his cigarette, with just the right pause to emphasize his summary point: "There's a lot of money to be made here."

I explained to him repeatedly that cold calling the white pages just didn't sound like something I felt called to do. There was something intrinsic about that task that didn't resonate. Maybe he enjoyed the challenge, but it just wasn't in my DNA.

He responded with a sympathetic, knowing nod; then another drag on the cigarette, followed by a gentlemanly sip from his Scotch on the rocks. This time, for added affect, he leaned forward slightly, lowered his voice and repeated: "There's a *lot* of money to be made here."

"Gee, I just don't think I would like the work," I repeated.

"I hear what you're saying," he said empathetically, and took another drag on the cigarette, which amazed me because he still hadn't exhaled the first two. "What I'm saying, is: there's a lot of *money* to be made here."

The Stallion couldn't envision anything but money motivating work. I've come to see this as a sign of someone who has yet to make peace with money. It's as though money is an enemy to be conquered. And as in war, one must eventually do things he or she rather wouldn't … like cold call the white pages.

Conventional wisdom assumes money is the primary motivator in job performance. Maybe that's not an assumption; maybe it's true. If so, it's a telling statement. To say this is not to be judgmental. I suspect many people look at money as the yardstick of career success because they have never been invited to look at their jobs in any other way. It's the only measure they know.

Farmers are a good example of how we *should* view our work. Every imaginable market force conspires against them. They produce commodities and by definition commodity prices are difficult to unilaterally increase because of a lack of differentiation between farmers' production. For example, whether a pasta maker is buying durum wheat from North Dakota or its competitors, as long as each producer meets certain milling standards the buyer has leverage. "North Dakota won't sell for $4 a bushel? Fine, I'll go to South Dakota, or Montana or Argentina if I have to." The baker, on the other hand, has much more leverage. You want the best loaf of ciabatta in town? Then you have to fork over $4.29 a loaf down at Breadsmith or other upscale bread store. Little does the consumer know that there is, literally, about a dime's worth of wheat in the loaf.

This is why farmers incessantly complain about prices. Yet they still borrow money each spring to put in a crop. Working sixteen-hour days, they gamble with weather, insects, and disease in the hope that they will beat the odds and be able to put food on their own table. The world owes them a huge debt of gratitude.

So why do they do it? If there is so much risk, and so slight a return — at least for the little guy — why stay in it?

Certainly the work is intrinsically life-giving. Every spring the farmer cooperates in a miracle of nature, watching seeds magically collect and organize — on their own, with no direction from him — water, minerals, air and sunshine and turn them into things we can eat.

Participating in this annual mystery makes farmers very reflective people. And it's this deeper reflection that keeps them on the farm despite the pay. Most farmers I've known find comfort in knowing they participate in one of the corporal acts of mercy: feeding the hungry. There is a satisfaction in work that goes beyond mere profits.

I contend that everyone, with even a minimum of reflection, could find deeper meaning in work. Take for example the airline flight attendant. With more than a million frequent-traveler miles, I've concluded that flight attendants actually have a lot in common with farmers: The pay is lousy, the hours long, and the work repetitive. And, like farmers, they would love to control the weather.

Given these parameters, flight attendants would find their work more satisfying if they understood it was about more than making money for a large corporation. In truth, their vocation is a service of enormous benefit to thousands of people each day.

Like farmers, flight attendants graciously perform their own corporal works of mercy. Every day they reunite fathers with their children, quietly carry the bereaved family, join lover with the beloved. There is much deeper meaning in their work than simply serving snacks and attending to safety issues. Ultimately, their work is about relationships. Flight attendants are part of an industry that unites people. Whether it's a family on vacation, or executives on business, air travel brings people together to play and work. Just try to imagine modern life without their service. Certainly the flight attendant who sees his or her work in this light finds daily annoyances easier to bear and work more satisfying, regardless of the paycheck.

Joy in labor remains unclaimed by millions, simply because, like The Stallion, they have not looked past money to the inherent value of work. I'm not discouraging ambition. Want a better job and more money? Good for you. I'm simply giving the same caution that a grandparent would give, with a bit of a twist. The elderly, having life experience under their belt, would say, "Love what you do." Good advice, but it stops short. "Love what you do" is still about *you*. Like money, it speaks to what *you* get out of the deal. I'm saying, "Even if you don't *like* what you do, find *meaning* in it until you can find something better, and find that meaning in discovering how it serves others."

This understanding looks outward. Adopt this attitude and the present work will be much more bearable, maybe even satisfying. If you don't, you are left with only the money, and there are millions of jobs in this country where that will be completely unsatisfying.

My friend Troy had one of those jobs. Five nights a week it was his job to clean a butcher shop. In particular, he described a machine outfitted with thousands of needles used to tenderize steaks. Imagine waking every morning knowing your day would end cleaning that same impossible machine. Yet, I never heard him complain. Instead he explained that his steaks were being distributed to restaurants throughout the state, and even a bit of meat left on the machine could endanger the health of thousands.

You would think he was saving the planet.

Imagine if we all adopted this same understanding of work's inherent worth. There is value in even the most unappealing of work, and Troy understood that. It got him through, night after night, until he found a better job. We could all learn something from Troy. If you want to make peace with money, you must discover in your work how it genuinely serves others.

6. *The person who has not made peace with money has a belief that, just for the money, we must do things we are not called to do.*

It's natural to want to better one's life. But it's important that each job or career change be done for the right reason, and that means making the change with consideration for more than money.

I wish I had recognized this earlier in life. When I finished my undergraduate degree in music education, I realized that I loved teaching, music, and kids. At the same time, I hated teaching music to kids. This may seem illogical. But then I love beer, ice cream, and dill pickles. I just don't want to eat them together.

So after finishing my undergraduate degree, I went back to work at the university golf course where I had been mowing grass for several summers. At my graduation party my godmother asked me, "Gregory, have you got a job now with your college degree?" She always used my formal name when she was particularly proud of me. And having prayed the Rosary several hundred times for her godchildren, she had every right to have high expectations.

"Yes, Aunty. I'm working for the university."

"Oh, you got a job as a music professor!" she naïvely assumed.

I didn't have the heart to set the record straight. At the same time I knew silence was an implicit lie, but didn't feel a graduation party was the time to get into the Bermuda Triangle of teaching-music-to-kids.

Anyway, I knew I could fend for myself, and wasn't going to be a burden on anyone. In preparation for graduation I had formed a band with some friends called The Skeptics, which was a perfect name because by June I began wondering whether we would ever get a paying gig. My hope was that by the time the golf course closed in October I would have found something to pay the bills.

And I did. Steve "The Suave" was getting the group Justin' Tyme back together and needed a bass player. By October I was booked every weekend. Suddenly I was a professional musician, living large in Grand Forks, North Dakota. Over the next five years I played in a number of bands, enjoyed it immensely, and earned enough to pay rent and buy groceries.

Then in 1989, at the age of 29, it finally became apparent that my employment trajectory didn't put me in the category of preferred husband material. My net income for the year was just over $11,000. So I borrowed some math books from the local middle school, boned up on algebra, and sat for the Graduate Management Admissions Test.

Getting into Notre Dame was the easy part. The transition from music to business was more difficult than I anticipated, requiring a different skill set. I can't say I enjoyed it. But I had borrowed $18,000 for the first year alone, so I was committed. By the time I graduated in 1991 the school debt grew to nearly $40,000. I was happy to know that starting salaries for MBAs that year averaged $36,000. So when Tom Suddes offered me a job as a development consultant, and asked about my salary requirements, I said $36,000. He agreed, and I went to work.

"Imagine that!" I thought to myself. With just two years of school I more than tripled my annual income. I was feeling pretty good until the end of the year. When I calculated my taxes I realized that of the $36,000 in gross income, Uncle Sam took about a third and student loans another third, leaving me with about $11,000. That number was eerily familiar. As a musician I worked four hours a night, took a break every 45 minutes to drink beer provided by my employer, and had a view from the stage better than any office in America. Now I was a consultant working sixty hours a week, all buttoned up, traveling four days a week (albeit to exotic locations like Cleveland) but netting the same amount of money. It felt like karmic payback for doing a good thing for the wrong reason. That is, education is never "wasted." It is intrinsically good. But my heart never felt at home in business the way it did in music. Though I had a knack for business and knew I would do well, I never honestly felt called to do it. I opted for Notre Dame and a career in business because I believed it was what a responsible person would naturally do: seek the material good.

I was not the only one at Notre Dame who made this mistake. During fall orientation I met a new classmate at a social and asked what he wanted to do after he finished his degree. He said he hoped to get a good job; he wasn't more specific than that. The job didn't matter. He just wanted to save up a lot of money, and then move to Montana to be a cowboy. So I asked him the next obvious question, "Why don't you just go be a cowboy?"

From the look on his face, I should have stopped there, but couldn't help myself. "By the time you make your first million, you'll be too old to ride."

Of course, his plan was bigger than just rounding up cattle. He wanted to make enough money to buy his own ranch. But the longer we talked, the less that made sense. He didn't want to be a businessman. He loved the outdoors, horses, and physical labor. Even if he finished his MBA, found a job on Wall Street, made his first million by age thirty and bought the Montana ranch of his dreams, what then? Did he want to manage a ranch, or be a cowboy?

Buying a ranch would bring with it all the financial worries that farmers face. It's an extremely risky business. Did he want to sit in the ranch office worrying about cattle futures, or live the life of the hired hands? Frankly, he wanted to be a cowboy. But he uncritically accepted the notion that we must do things we are not called to do, just for the money.

When you're young and make this mistake, it's very forgivable. When you're older, and know better, it's so common there's a nickname for this phenomenon: golden handcuffs. Sadly, many people discover later in life that the career they chose for financial security was not properly discerned. It may have made logical sense at the time, but was never a decision of the heart. Yet their lifestyle and financial commitments, even their standing in social circles, makes it difficult to return to their true calling. Like a well worn shoe, the erroneous belief that "money" is more important than "calling" leaves them — note the irony — ill at peace with money.

7. *The person who has not made peace with money feels grave discomfort when asked for alms.*

This uneasiness manifests itself in a variety of ways. Some people work hard to avoid being asked. Others direct the topic away from themselves by generously referring *others* who ought to be the ones to give. Still others preempt the conversation by explaining how dire their circumstances are. Some artfully combine all three.

****

If you see within yourself any of these seven signs and symptoms, welcome to the human race. Making peace with money on a spiritual level is no easy task. But it can be done. In chapter 3 we begin to apply the medicine.

FOR REFLECTION

1. Review the seven symptoms of the person not at peace with money.

2. Note the ones that apply to your life and circumstance. Be painstakingly honest with yourself. Ask the Holy Spirit to help you see yourself truthfully.

3. For each one that applies to you, summarize in three sentences how this symptom manifests itself in your life. Use actual examples. The act of writing it down is important, because it will force you to find words for what you are feeling.

4. Share what you have written with a close friend or spouse. For these and subsequent exercises at the end of chapters, you will benefit more fully if you have someone with whom to share your thoughts — a "money partner."

Chapter 3

The Prescription

These days there are plenty of people promising financial freedom and offering guidance on how to obtain more or spend less. On a practical level, much of this advice can be helpful but it will always be insufficient because it points our gaze outward, at the acquisition of money, and this is not where financial freedom is found. As demonstrated earlier, acquiring wealth — even significant wealth — does not necessarily free one from financial worries. Rather, freedom can only be found by looking inward, and begins with a question: "How generous am I?"

At first glance, this may seem odd. Most of us are looking for ways to make more money, not give away the little we have. Still, I've known people who achieved peace in money matters, and others who have not. Inevitably, financial freedom does not come from what we possess, but from a willingness to joyfully share.

This is the kind of uncomplicated truth mothers teach their children; the kind of truth we try to escape as we age. Adulthood comes with the power to reason, and we often employ those powers in an attempt to wrestle free of truth, to replace it with something less demanding. In this case, we're tempted to question mother's childhood advice and point out: "To be generous requires wealth. If

I had enough wealth to be generous, I wouldn't have to worry about money!"

The erroneous assumption illustrated in this statement is that generosity is only the purview of the wealthy, that it becomes an option and obligation only when one has attained a certain amount of wealth. Nothing could be further from the truth. Generosity, and the financial freedom it brings, is a disposition of the soul. Both rich and poor can be generous; both can be greedy. *Generosity has virtually no connection with one's wealth.*

How can this be? How is it possible to be greedy if you have little or nothing to give away?

An illustration may help. I recently visited a big-box office supply store in search of a new desk. I reviewed several models on my own, decided on one I liked, and knew I could assemble it if I could get it home. That left just one small problem. Would the shipping container fit in the trunk of my car?

It took some time to get the attention of a clerk who then only called a warehouse attendant. When he appeared several minutes later, I explained that I needed the dimensions of the box containing the desk so that I could determine whether it would fit in my car. Rolling his eyes, he walked me back to the furniture display. Without a word, he pointed to the dimensions clearly listed on the display.

"That's the dimensions of the desk once it's assembled," I countered. "I need to know the dimensions of the box."

He shrugged. "Can't help you," he said nonchalantly.

I was a bit surprised by the brevity of his answer. "Why not?"

"Don't have a tape measure," he explained as he walked away.

It seems an office supply superstore would carry a ruler in its inventory. Or if nothing else, an 8 ½-by-11-inch sheet of paper could substitute as a measuring tool for an estimate. But I had no way of getting into the warehouse to take the measurements myself, so I decided to leave.

As I was heading for the door, another clerk — named Mohamed and a recent immigrant from Africa — spotted me and offered to help. I recounted the exchange with the first clerk, and was told apologetically, "He's just like that." Within minutes Mohamed returned with the dimensions of the box, and I made the purchase.

It's probably safe to assume that neither of these two clerks was wealthy. Yet one was greedy, the other generous. More precisely, the first clerk was lazy, but laziness is simply another form of greed related to sharing one's time and energy. In a sense, laziness, a lack of concern for others, or self-centeredness are all manifestations of greed. Thus, it's fair to say it is possible to be greedy, even if you don't have great wealth.

This brings up an important point. Because greed is fundamentally a disposition of the soul, it isn't limited to Wall Street bankers and corporate executives. Even entry-level employees can choose to act out of a spirit of greed or a spirit of generosity. The first clerk couldn't care less whether he made a sale. His actions spoke loud and clear: he was only in it for himself and the paycheck. The customer? Nothing but trouble! The company? Not his concern! His attitude was little more than thinly disguised greed. Unlike the second clerk, he certainly did not exhibit the characteristics of a generous person willing to give of himself.

So don't assume that greed and generosity are issues only for the rich. The inordinate desire to amass wealth may be the first thing that comes to mind when we think of greed, but it's just one manifestation of the illness. As we've already seen, laziness is another. Even something as small as turning a blind eye to the needs of one's spouse is, properly understood, rooted in greed that asks, "What do *I* get out of this?" In contrast, generosity asks, "What does the *other* get out of this?" These two questions fundamentally define the difference between greed and generosity, character issues with which every human, rich and poor alike, must wrestle. We each choose to be either greedy or generous with what we have, even if all we have is our time, talent, and energy.

Perhaps you have never thought of greed as an issue for both rich and poor. It is tempting to force the charge only upon the wealthy — because most of us are not wealthy! That way we sidestep the need to examine our own behavior. For example, in the case of our store clerks, there may be a tendency to forgive the lack of interest of the first employee. It could be argued that low wages and lack of benefits create just this attitude. That may be true. But do two wrongs make a right? Let's give the curt young man the benefit of the doubt. Let's assume that he had little concern for the customer because his employer had little concern for him. In other words, the young man did not act out of a spirit of generosity because his boss showed none of the same spirit toward him. Even so, is it right to react to greed by adopting a greedy attitude?

Perhaps our first clerk believes that nonservice is a way of "sticking it to the man." But who is "the man"? Who is this employee hoping to hurt through his surly attitude and nonperformance of duties? It could very well include thousands of pensioners who hold the company's stock in their mutual funds, who rely on its performance for their living expenses. It also includes his peers, who depend on the company's profitability for their livelihood.

Ultimately, who suffers the most from the first clerk's attitude? Obviously, it cost me a half hour of frustration, and it nearly cost the store a sale. But it's costing that young man much more. He's spending his life weighed down by a disposition of the soul he may not even recognize. Yet others do. As Mohamed pointed out, "He's just like that."

Unfortunately, this attitude easily deteriorates into a justification for employee theft, a national problem that forces prices up for rich and poor alike. In 2008, one out of every thirty employees was apprehended for theft from their employer.[7] And the theft was more than office supplies. "On a per case average, dishonest employees steal a little over seven times the amount stolen by shoplifters."[8] Imagine the adverse effect hundreds of like-minded employees have on the corporation and the families it employs. The collective impact of dishonest employees might easily equal that of any corrupt CEO.

In this light I find it puzzling that vilifying corporate executives has become so fashionable of late. Too many of those pointing fingers share the same sinful inclination, but do not see the collective impact of an otherwise insignificant act. Viewed from the heavens, greed is greed. And given a chance, the store clerk who would pilfer merchandise would likely embezzle millions as CEO. A thief is a thief. There is no difference between the two except the size of the illicit opportunity.

"But wait," you may say. "Certainly pilfering merchandise is not the same as a multimillion dollar scam?" True, there is a difference in *degree*, but not in the *essential features*. To illustrate the distinction between the two, we turn to a story from the farm.

My father-in-law had a dairy herd of about one hundred cows. Since they eat several hundred pounds of hay each day, the herd produces several hundred pounds of "product" other than milk. Throughout the week it's necessary to use a small skid-steer tractor to push the waste into a pit, where it is pumped to a 100-by-200-foot clay-lined lagoon north of the farm.

There manure and rain water collect and decompose until October, when the lagoon is emptied. It's not a pleasant task. A tractor with a portable pump is backed to the edge of the lagoon, and then an intake pipe is settled into the gooey mix so that it can be pumped onto the "honey wagon" and spread upon the fields. The process takes several days.

On one occasion the discharge pump on the wagon failed in the middle of the field, leaving my father-in-law with nearly three thousand gallons of liquid manure and no way to spread it. To make the needed repairs, he would have to first empty the tank. Without stopping to consider that he was on the downhill side of the tank, he wrenched opened the relief valve. Within seconds, the force of the liquid showered him head to toe, filling his pockets and nearly knocking him to the ground.

Here we pause for a rhetorical question. Which would you prefer: (1) stay away from the honey wagon's spray, (2) have manure only up to your waist, or (3) have your entire body showered with it? If you chose (2) or (3), there is a difference in *degree* of the offense; one is worse than the other. But there is no difference in the *essential features*. Whether covered to the waist, or showered head to toe, you are still dealing with the same dung. Either situation is one to avoid.

With this illustration in mind, let's return to our question: is there a difference between a clerk stealing merchandise and a corporate officer defrauding customers or the company? There is a difference in *degree*, but not the *essential features* of the act: whether you steal ten dollars or one million dollars, you're still a thief. Like the honey wagon, it's something to avoid altogether.

Here's my point: like the lazy or dishonest store clerk, there is a temptation in all of us to dismiss the minor infraction. But imagine saying, "I'm taking off my shoes and socks to go wading in the lagoon. Want to come? I'm only planning to go up to my knees." Who would accept that invitation? Would you find any amount of manure spread on your body acceptable? What if it's just a little on your hands? Would you serve dinner thinking, "This little bit isn't going to hurt anyone." Or would you want to cleanse your hands, right down to the nails?

Greed is like that lagoon. Whether slipping and going under, wading at the edges, or getting a little under the nails, it's still a thing to be entirely avoided. So why are we so eager to dismiss the minor infraction in ourselves? Whether rich or poor, no one is exempt from the struggle between generosity and greed. As long as we live, the interior battle must be waged, even in the little things in life.

Generosity and greed are both issues of the *soul*, so they must be addressed on a *spiritual* level. That's why no money magazine, despite the promises, can give you real financial freedom. If you are to overcome persistent worries about money, it will only happen when you address generosity and greed on a spiritual level. Anything else is merely cosmetic.

So what must we do to begin?

The starting point for all spiritual growth is humility, the willingness to examine our actions and motivations without pretense, *even in the small interactions of daily life.* That's no small feat. I'm sad to admit I still find plenty of greed in my own behavior.

On Divine Mercy Sunday — the Sunday after Easter — my wife brought home a dozen donuts to continue the Eastertide celebration. As she prepared brunch, I snuck a peek at the selection, hoping to find my favorite. Sure enough, it was there, but only one of twelve: my beloved maple iced, the crown jewel of the donut kingdom.

I knew the donuts were intended for dessert, but I couldn't help myself. What if someone else claimed the maple iced? The selection left a lot to be desired. It was mostly kid stuff. What if I ended up with a jelly-filled, or worse yet, a chocolate with sprinkles?

So I reverted to my old ways. Like my brothers and I used to do, I laid claim to the maple iced by taking a rather large bite out of it and returning it to the box. "There," I thought, "Problem solved. No one will want that one now."

It was an ideal solution. It's not like I was taking the *whole* donut, putting it on a plate wrapped in plastic with my name on it. That wouldn't be proper. After all, Stella made the trip to the donut shop; she should have first pick. Not allowing her to choose first would be, well, not very generous. So by returning the donut to the box, I avoided that problem. At the same time, I knew no one would pick a donut with teeth marks. By any standards, it was a brilliant move.

I wish this weren't a true story. It illustrates one of those ever-so-small incidents that we dismiss in our own behavior every day, like stealing a parking spot or not holding the elevator for the gentlemen just twenty steps away. We rationalize those little, stray acts of self-centeredness. Have you stopped to notice? It never ceases to amaze me how selfishness, even in insignificant acts of human failure, continues to sprout in the soul. It's like a garden that must be constantly tended, lest the weeds overtake the good fruit.

Rather than examine ourselves on this level of day-to-day interaction, there is a tendency to erect within ourselves all sorts of walls and protections so that we need not look at what needs conversion. And should our defenses crumble, and we begin to see our weakness and express a sense of guilt, there is no shortage of voices assuring us we are fine just the way we are. Why? For the same reason that drunks want others to drink with them: to justify their own behavior. As long as others are doing it too, it can't be *that* bad. In short, there are plenty of people quick to excuse our behavior because they want the same favor in return.

As a result, it's hard to hear our better angels. Left to our own devices, with no one to hold us accountable, we slowly, imperceptibly, justify an ever-increasing range of behaviors. Without humility, it becomes easier with each passing year to dismiss the quiet voice of our conscience. Life begins to deteriorate. Thankfully, when things get bad enough, and we're perhaps finally open to a little help, God intervenes with an offer. *It is at this point that grace can literally save us from ourselves.*

Grace is a supernatural share in the divine life of God. This is quite a concept to grasp — the notion that we humans can share in the animating breath of the Spirit of God. Though entire treatises could be written on grace, let it suffice to think of grace as a supernatural aid that moves us toward goodness. More plainly, we might envision grace as God saying, "This path is better for you. Will you let me help?" Through people and circumstance, God invites us to see life in a new way, to see ourselves more honestly, and to acknowledge our sinfulness alongside our goodness. He invites, and then awaits a response. In theological parlance, this invitation and our response are known as the "divine economy." In layman's terms, it's "the way God works."

God intervenes in our lives constantly. Not in the sense that he forces: love does not impose. Rather, we are offered a never-ending series of invitations that await our cooperation. Even though burdened with self-deception, we can hope to learn humility because we are aided from on high. Take away grace, and the outcome would surely be less promising.

God's grace comes when least expected. I recall meeting my wife's paternal grandmother for the first time several years ago. Ida, now deceased, lived in Strasburg, North Dakota, home of the town's favorite son and musician, Lawrence Welk. Like nearly all the residents of that part of the state, Ida was a German-from-Russia, a group that emigrated first from Germany to Russia, then from Russia to the United States: thus the German-from-Russia moniker. They were among the last immigrant groups to homestead in this country, and what was left by the late 1890s was not premium farmland. For many on the northern plains, it meant a claim to the semi-arid, rocky ground of south central North Dakota.

Imagine the fortitude required to lay claim to a windswept plot of prairie, to homestead on land that may or may not produce a crop, where sod was the only material available to build shelter, where winter could drop to minus thirty degrees Fahrenheit and summers reach over one hundred with not even a tree to give shade.

Climate was not the only hardship. In Russia the people lived in small villages, and farmers would go out to the surrounding fields each day, but return in the evening to the support of their community. Not in America. In its wisdom, the government required homesteaders to live on the land they claimed. This meant crushing isolation for pioneers courageous enough to test nature. Reading the diaries of the first settlers, isolation seems to have been just as burdensome as toiling the rock-strewn prairie.

This was Ida's lineage, and her people's history of endurance is reflected even in their bare-bones cuisine. There are dozens of recipes that use just five basic ingredients: flour, water, salt, cream, and vinegar. That's a rather somber grocery list. Soon after I married into the clan, I concluded — only half-joking — that the German-Russian attitude toward meals was the same as their stoic approach to life: to make it through with as little ancillary pleasure as possible.

Ida did not have an easy life. Her husband died of cancer just a few months after the youngest child, now my father-in-law, was born, leaving Ida to farm 360 acres and raise five children on her own. Her brother Nick, who had ten children, occupied the neighboring farmstead. At the funeral he told Ida not to worry: they would raise the children together. A few months later, Nick also succumbed to cancer, leaving his wife and Ida to fend for themselves. Imagine the daily struggle: two women, two farms, and fifteen children.

They were capable women. Somehow they managed, and the experience of those early years left an imprint on their character. Years later, Ida gave Stella and me five pounds of sugar and a sack of flour as a wedding gift. I don't recall adding those items (or vinegar, cream, or salt) to the wedding registry, but to Ida I'm sure such a gift made perfect sense. Staple foods would get a young couple through at least the first month of marriage.

If memory serves me, Ida said she left the state just twice in her life. She didn't much care for travel, especially to big cities like Minneapolis, and found those that made such trips a bit strange. "People come back from these trips and tell me, 'I was scared the whole time,'" recounted Ida. "I tell them, 'Then why do you go?'"

Such was Ida's straightforward logic. She was always kind, but never one to butter your ego or allow any puffery to slip past. She was just the kind of simple soul God loves to use.

One day I was trying to explain to Ida my work as a development consultant. Knowing her preference for straight talk, I thought I was doing a pretty good job of explaining what I did on a daily basis, without sounding self-important. That's when grace intervened. I still recall that sweet, squeaky little voice, as her eyes finally lit up with understanding. "Oh you're a professional beggar!"

My wife Stella, sitting beside me, had a good laugh. Most of the humor likely came from the expression on my face. With a brief word, Ida stripped me of all pretense, *even that of which I was formerly unaware.* This frail, elderly woman, who only once or twice in her life had left the state, knew exactly what I was: a beggar.

This is how grace works. Ida's words came entirely out of the blue, an invitation from God for me to rethink what I was about, who I was, and what I did. Now it was up to me to respond. I could have walked away that afternoon and arrogantly dismissed her comments, as though that might have been possible having come from a saintly soul like Ida. Or I could have embraced her words, let them settle inside me, and consider whether they had any validity.

I chose the latter. I opened myself to the grace that flowed through Ida. And since that day I am pleased to wear the title she offered me. I've dressed it up a bit; I now refer to myself as a "mendicant." This sounds a bit classier than beggar. But I know what I am.

This choice of words will come as anathema to my peers in the development consulting profession. They have spent years trying to convince development staffers that we are not begging for money, we are asking people for an investment in a social good. Very well. I understand that line of reasoning. Still, Ida was on to something: I have reverted to the concept of begging alms because there is a fatal flaw in the idea of charity as an investment.

That's the subject of the next chapter.

FOR REFLECTION

As children, my brothers and I were taught to conclude each day with an examination of conscience. Today some may be uncomfortable with the practice, but in retrospect it's a habit I regret having let slip in my teens and twenties. How does one grow in character without a daily self-assessment?

Before continuing on to the next chapter, it would be helpful to experience this practice, especially as it pertains to the topic at hand — generosity. This evening set aside fifteen minutes free of distractions. No TV, no music, no Internet.

1. Ask yourself these questions:
    a. Was I generous today with my time?
    b. Was I short with anyone?

c. Is there anyone with whom I need to make amends?

d. Did I find myself wishing ill on another? Why?

e. Have I ever accused someone else, even if only in my thoughts, of being greedy?

f. Have I ever been less than generous with my time or money?

2. Summarize your answers in writing. Use actual examples. The act of writing it down is important because it will help you to be honest with yourself. It will also force you to find words for what you are feeling.

3. If you want to benefit more fully from the exercise, share these thoughts with your "money partner," spouse, or close friend.

Chapter 4

Giving as a Spiritual Act

It has become fashionable among fund-raisers to use the word "investment" when asking people to support a charity. There is something to be said about this viewpoint. By speaking of gifts as an investment, it suggests that those receiving the money will use it efficiently to effect some positive, measurable change.

For example, a charity might suggest to a prospective donor that an investment of ten thousand dollars will underwrite training for a half dozen individuals in a new skill, thus permanently relieving the government of welfare expenses for six families, which could be considerably more than ten thousand dollars. Seen in this light, the gift is arguably a good "investment." To speak of a return on investment suggests that the gift will have the intended impact. Ultimately, it speaks to good stewardship.

This is important. With so much human suffering, it is unethical for charities to spend money foolishly, to waste the dollars given in good faith by donors. At the same time, there is a serious flaw in the idea of charity as a mere investment: *it strips the act of its inherent spiritual dimension*. It debases it. Correctly understood, giving alms is a fundamentally spiritual act, a response to the invitation of grace. To see it as mere investment brings it down to the level of consumerism. At its worse, it invites the donor to ask, "What am I getting for my money?" In a sense, giving becomes just one more purchase.

There is a better way to think about our giving.

Consider two approaches. In the first, we regard our donations as an investment, as illustrated above. There are certainly plenty of charities asking for our help. If a particular charity passes muster — if the organization can prove its effectiveness — then they earn a green light and a donation.

At first glance, this may seem reasonable. We expect charities to be good stewards of our gifts. But do you see what's happening here? In viewing our donations as an investment, we essentially set ourselves up as a sort of judge. We are the interrogators, in a manner of speaking. After all, it's our money. We'll ask the questions.

This approach is very common. For example, when parishes need to improve or add to facilities, public opinion among the congregants often requires the pastor to justify every expense. With a little imagination, you can hear the faithful. "Are you sure the roof is leaking? Do we really need new shingles? Can't we just get three good men up on the roof with a bucket of tar? And what's wrong with the shag carpet in the rectory? I heard avocado and gold are coming back into style!"

Of course, parishioners have a right to expect their pastor to make wise spending decisions. That's perfectly acceptable and not the issue here. The problem is almsgiving that begins and ends with the would-be donor acting as judge. Gifts given with this attitude leave little room for God to work with us.

Consider, then, a better way to give. God places good and holy desires on the human heart. Before judging the worthiness of a charity, what if we first allowed God to interrogate *us*, then gave him permission to lead our decisions? Rather than play judge, what if we handed that role over to God, asking, "What would you have me do with my wealth?" I contend that we would be much more unsparing and joyful in our giving.

This is what I mean when I speak of a spiritual approach to giving. It begins with looking inward and discovering the invitation to generosity God has written on the human heart. We all have it. To use a philosophical term, this inclination is part of human nature. Throughout all cultures, and throughout human history, generosity has been recognized and revered as an innate good. C. S. Lewis alludes to this in *Mere Christianity*, when he describes the concept of Natural Law. He argues that certain qualities of character are instinctively admired independent of culture, religion, or time: courage, generosity, self-sacrificial love. It's as though we are hardwired for these virtues. Even individuals who don't exhibit them in their personal lives still admire them in others. We instinctively know generosity is a good thing. And we know it because the invitation comes not from our own intellect, but from God. Our proper response, then, is not to our own intellect but to God himself. It's a spiritual response to a spiritual invitation.

If we give alms with the attitude of an investment, we may feel satisfaction. But if we allow God to first examine us, then give him permission to lead our decisions, we find liberating joy. There's a difference between the two:

satisfaction emanates from within us, but joy emanates from God. It is here that you will find the seeds of freedom from worries about money.

If you spent any time as a child in religious education classes, you likely heard the saying, "All good things come from God." But as an adult have you considered what this means, how it plays out on a practical level? Many interpret this saying to mean that all our material possessions ultimately come from God, and they would be right. But it doesn't end there. Have you ever heard a small voice in your head encouraging you to lose weight, quit smoking, or visit your ailing, older relatives? That too comes from God. Feel an inclination to apologize, make amends, or hold your tongue? All these are invitations from God to respond to grace; so too is the interior prompting to give of time and money. Generosity is a spiritual act precisely because it is a response to God's invitation. Through an exercise of free will, we cooperate in God's work: our gifts feed the hungry, house the homeless, and do all manner of good works.

At least that is how it is meant to be: a freely chosen response. Recall the "divine economy" discussed in Chapter 3. God invites but never coerces: forced generosity is a contradiction in terms.

Forced generosity? Does such a thing exist? In many subtle ways it does, and it's actually not that uncommon. Sometimes we give because the boss asked. In other cases, it might be undue pressure from a pastor or a desire to save face in our social circle. There are all kinds of influence that render our giving less than free. While those pressures may benefit a charity in the short term, they have an unintended side effect not in keeping with God's plan.

Consider the impact on the heart in these two scenarios, one in which the gift — in this case, time — is given freely, and other in which it is not. For our first example, we turn to those high schools and religious education programs that require service hours of their students. The hope, of course, is that by mandating "volunteer" service, students will develop a concern for others.

There may be some value in this approach, to the degree that they expose students to those less fortunate. But does it have the intended effect? Does it lead to conversion of heart? That's the real test: conversion. Does mandatory volunteerism cause a deep change in young peoples' hearts? Does it help them discover the joy of self-sacrificial love? It may for some if they go on to give of themselves when the mandate is no longer there. That's why these programs still exist: we win a few. But for the majority, I fear the activity remains just a dutiful commitment.

In contrast, consider those instances when young people discover the invitation to generosity God has written on their hearts, and respond of their own free will. In this scenario, service is marked by joy and enthusiasm. I saw this dynamic firsthand in the spring of 2009. In April, a record flood threatened Fargo, North Dakota, and the city had just five days to fill and lay three million sandbags. If you do the math, you can appreciate the challenge. At forty pounds per sandbag, citizens needed to move one hundred and twenty million pounds of sand *four times*: to make the sandbag, stack it on a pallet, unload it at the site, and finally lay it on the levee — all in five days. Considering the four steps, that's nearly *half a billion* pounds of sand moved by hand. With ninety-one thousand residents, including children, pensioners and nursing mothers, the odds didn't look good. But the volunteer response was overwhelming, especially among college students. I worked a couple of night shifts alongside them, and was astounded at their zeal. Quite literally, it was the young who saved the city.

Imagine the same scenario, this time with young adults conscripted to service. Would we have had the same number of young people? Maybe. But I doubt I would have seen such selflessness and good cheer, and I doubt the young would have experienced the grace and joy so evident that week. There is a significant difference between students *discovering* their innate desire to serve others and *forcing* them to give of their time unwillingly. The flood presented an occasion for young people to lift their souls toward God through service to man. Had the work been mandated, it would have come crashing to earth as merely the unwilling fulfillment of a social contract.

This illustrates the central point I'm trying to make: the attitude engendered in the heart of one who gives willingly is quite different from the attitude of one required to comply with a mandate. For an act to be a generous one, for it to rise to the level of a spiritual act, it must be rooted in free will.

This is why giving alms to the poor — an act of free will — is entirely different from taxing individuals for the same needs. One is voluntary, the other not. One responds to the promptings of grace, the other to the demands of government. If you want to experience the spiritual benefits of almsgiving, you must give alms freely and without reservation. No amount of taxes can replace almsgiving.

Please don't misread the point at hand. I am making no judgment here about tax policy, how much is enough or too little. That is a political and financial question. Our purpose is to understand man's *spiritual* relationship toward money and possessions. We want to examine the effect on the heart when money is given freely and the consequences when it is not.

Unfortunately, few people have ever thought deeply about the distinction between alms and taxes. It has become fashionable for some politicians to associate lower taxes with greed and higher taxes with an act of generosity. This sounds reasonable at first glance, but ultimately does not pass the test of reason. *By definition, paying taxes can never be a generous act because it is not an act of free will.* Forcing people through taxes to relinquish wealth may be necessary, even patriotic, but do not make the mistake of equating it with generosity.

There are four ways free will plays a central role in how alms and taxes each affect the human heart.

1. Almsgiving softens the heart, while taxes tempt an opposite response.

As a solicitor of alms, I've seen the process a thousand times. The invitation is made, causing discomfort and restlessness within the soul. But after a period of reflection, grace aids a generous response, an act of free will. The result? The donor feels joy, the same kind of happiness that one experiences when choosing patience over rudeness, kindness over harsh words, a salad rather than the bacon-cheeseburger. Having sided with our better angels, having cooperated with God's invitation to generosity, there is a certain spiritual consolation — even for those who do not yet recognize it as such. In contrast, it's very possible to relinquish one's personal wealth through taxes for equally noble purposes, and be left feeling not consolation but bitterness.

2. Giving alms usually is accompanied by a sincere concern about those served by the gift.

The connection between donor and recipient does not begin and end with writing the check. It continues. The donor wants to know what happened. Have things improved? Did my gift make a difference in someone's life? Through our voluntary financial support we enter into the lives of others. Part of one's heart is invested, hoping to see a specific good come about. Put another way, there is a joy in the desire to do good that accompanies the gift. Contrast this with the experience of paying taxes. Did you feel these same sentiments last April 15?

3. The concern on the part of the donor engenders a sense of community.

People sometimes give to broad causes, but more frequently they give to other people. Witness the effectiveness of appeals targeted to help a specific person, such as World Vision that asks donors to sponsor a child. Almsgiving entails the spiritual benefit of creating a *sense of community* with those our dollars help. It makes real the notion that we are all God's children, and bridges the artificial separation of so much of modern society.

In contrast, it's very possible to pay taxes and feel no connection whatsoever with the recipients of our tax dollars. In fact, instead of building community, taxes tempt the very opposite response. Rather than see one community of Americans, we come to envision ourselves in terms of givers and takers. One nation is replaced by two camps. Worse still, we walk past homeless beggars without compassion, justified in the knowledge that "we pay taxes to take care of that sort of thing." Chalk it up to unintended consequences: our taxes inadvertently give us an excuse to sidestep caring for our fellow man, one-on-one, in a personal way. No need to be a Good Samaritan. We pay government employees to take care of such things for us.

4. Almsgiving does what taxes cannot: it slowly changes the character of the donor by building trust in God's providence.

In a very earthy way, giving alms — especially when our own finances seem tight — requires an act of faith that God will care for our material needs. Forced to rely on God, those who embrace generosity slowly discover that God does indeed provide. Step by step we learn to trust, and each response to grace opens the door to yet more grace. *Eventually, with eyes fixed on God, he frees us of constant financial anxiety.*

In comparing almsgiving with taxes, I'm making no political statement. I readily admit that taxes are necessary in any form of government. Rather, I'm simply stating the obvious: taxes will never be a substitute for true generosity. Taxes and almsgiving have very different effects on the soul. The gift given freely comes with spiritual solicitude; the coerced "gift" does not. In the end, mandated taxes, even those earmarked for noble purposes, *deprive the giver of the spiritual benefits that would have come if he had given the money freely.*

This is my primary concern — the individual who will never experience the spiritual consolations that come with true charity. Imagine the thousands of Americans who dutifully pay their taxes and then forego giving to charity, having been led to believe they have done their part for God and country. What spiritual benefit is there in an act that is mandated? There is none, any more than one finds spiritual merit in a forced conversion. Unless these poor souls learn the distinction between paying taxes and giving alms, they will forever be deprived of an occasion of grace.

****

Unfortunately, many people do not understand the spiritual difference between taxes and alms.

My wife and I recently dined at a small Italian restaurant in Takoma Park, Maryland, one of the more modest suburbs northeast of Washington, D.C. It was a cozy eatery, with tables just a few feet from each other, the kind of arrangement that invites acknowledgment of one's neighbors, if only a "good evening."

We had just finished dinner when a forty-something couple was seated at a table next to us. If it's possible to have a distinguished, yet cotton-comfortable look, they had it — the kind of people you might want for neighbors. She had close-cropped hair and one of those long, intelligent faces so common on the East Coast. I just knew she had a vocabulary peppered with words like "anecdotal," "problematic," and (my favorite) "research indicates." She was not an unattractive woman, though she did look like she could use a good meal of buffalo, which, unfortunately for her, was not on the menu.

I don't recall much about the woman's husband. I'm pretty good with faces, but I honestly remember nothing about his appearance. He had somehow mastered an invisible quality that would make him difficult to pick out of a police lineup. Maybe he was CIA.

Since we were done eating, and they had not yet begun, it seemed appropriate to share a bit of polite conversation, especially given the awkwardness of the close quarters. Catching the gentleman's eye, I explained that we were new to the area, looking for a place to live, and considering an apartment in Takoma Park. I inquired as to whether they were from the immediate area. Who better to consult than one of the locals?

As it turns out, they were very happy in Takoma Park. Both worked in the area, she as a social worker and he as a union organizer. When he discovered we were from North Dakota, he congratulated us on electing very fine representatives to Washington.

I immediately began to feel uneasy. During the presidential election, Stella had been assaulted in Washington, D.C., by strangers not once, but twice, for wearing the wrong campaign button. We had agreed that no candidate was worth that kind of abuse, and vowed not to talk politics as long as we lived there. Still, I've known

Stella fifteen years and doubted she could resist the invitation to political discourse implicit in the gentleman's compliment, one he thought benign.

It wasn't Stella I was concerned about, however. It was the unsuspecting couple. When she senses hypocrisy, Stella is like a Dakota thunderstorm. On the horizon it's beautiful — lots of big, white, puffy clouds basking in the afternoon sun. An hour later it's blowing your granary over.

The waitress stopped by, and I asked for the check, hoping to pay the bill in time to avoid the storm. No such luck. It was as if this couple couldn't wait to announce their solidarity with America's poor, and soon were advocating for higher taxes. That was all the invitation Stella needed.

"How much more would you like to pay?" Stella asked oh-so-innocently.

The question caught them off guard. I gave Stella a pleading look, but it was already too late. She had picked up the scent, and the hunt was underway.

"Well, I don't know," the woman responded sheepishly. "I've never thought about how much."

Stella, always the helpful one, was quick to offer advice. "If you want to give more, you can," she announced cheerily. "The government has a special account that you can give to."

A look of panic came over our poor neighbor's face. "Well, the amount that I could send would do little good. Everyone has to pay more."

Following the lead of my better angels, I had resisted joining the repartee. But now I felt hopelessly tempted to tag-team the lady. Edging my way back into the conversation, I reminded her that it is better to light a single candle than to curse the darkness.

Even as the words were leaving my mouth, I knew I had gone too far. To use Scripture as sport is doubly sinister, and the "gotcha" intent immediately came back to haunt me. Feeling a need to repent, I quickly changed the subject.

"What would you like to see accomplished, if more money were available?" I queried.

She looked thankful that I was turning the conversation away from her personal generosity, and back toward a more generic topic. She explained that something needed to be done for the millions of Americans who don't have health insurance. There certainly was a need, I agreed. Sensing sincerity in her heart, I enthusiastically told her about my cousin in Salt Lake City that started a free clinic for the poor. Then, forgetting my momentary repentance, I was suddenly back to my old self. "If you want to write down your email address," I offered, "I will send information so you can donate."

Now I saw real panic. These questions were a mirror, and the woman was caught off guard by what she saw. She sincerely believed in her own virtue, in wanting to help the poor. That made her feel good. However, it was becoming apparent that she preferred someone else pay for it, making her advocacy a bit hollow. Thankfully, our bill came, redirecting our attention. We left without pressing for a response.

There are several things this exchange makes clear. First, that I'm a sinner. I will no doubt spend a good portion of the afterlife serving this couple dinner in repayment for the gleeful discomfort I caused. Moreover, there is also a high probability of spending the rest of *this* life doing dishes for my wife, for simply relaying the story.

But purgatory and dishpan hands aside, I decided to share this brief narrative because it illustrates how difficult it is to acknowledge one's true attitude toward money. There is nothing new here. In his epistle, James poses a question to first-century Christians. "If a brother or sister is poorly clothed and in lack of daily food, and one of you says to them, 'Go in peace, be warmed and filled,' without giving them the things needed for the body, what does it profit?" (Jas 2:15–16).

Two millennia later, circumstances have changed, but not human nature. Oddly, today there is no shortage of people who count it to their personal merit to simply advocate that *others* give more. To paraphrase James, what is the good of that? Such advocacy only has merit when we have first given freely from our own means. That's the true starting point. And when we give, it will only have spiritual consolation if we first turn to God and ask, "What would you have me do?"

This is what it means to give spiritually.

FOR REFLECTION

This chapter covered a lot of ground. Let's come to some conclusions.

1. When we give, it is reasonable to look at the effectiveness of an organization to ensure that our

money is well used. But to stop at this point is to miss the spiritual roots of our charity.

- The desire to be generous is written on the human heart.
- It is an invitation from God to participate in his work.
- In this light, we don't give just because someone else needs our help; we give because it is an occasion of grace, an opportunity to play a part in the Divine Plan.

2. As with all things God does, there is always an invitation, but never coercion. Love doesn't do that.

3. When we give alms, we experience four spiritual consolations:

- A softening of the heart and an experience of joy
- A sincere and ongoing concern about those served by the gift
- A sense of communion both with those our money aids, and with other donors who are also trying to help
- A change in character. Those who practice the virtue of generosity slowly discover that God does indeed provide. Each step in faith opens the door to yet more grace. *Eventually, God blesses us with a new attitude toward money that*

frees us from constant financial anxiety. This is, perhaps, the most profound benefit of almsgiving.

4. For an act of charity to merit these spiritual consolations, it must be rooted in free will. If giving is coerced — either through social pressure, a pastor's words that engender guilt, or tax code threatening fine and imprisonment — the giving of one's wealth loses its spiritual meaning. From this spiritual perspective, taxes can never replace the need to give alms, even if both are used for equally noble purposes.

****

1. In 250 words or less, describe how you feel about almsgiving. Do you ever feel obligated? By what or whom? If so, what could you do so that your almsgiving was truly an act of free will?

2. For the full benefit of this exercise, discuss your written answer with your money partner.

Chapter 5

Finding the Right God

Since we're approaching the halfway mark in this book, it might be a good time take stock of the ground already covered. How is it possible to overcome worries about money? I offered these observations:

1. Money cures some of our financial worries, but wealth alone is not the answer. Some individuals have great wealth, yet still worry constantly about money; others with little seem not to worry at all. Surely, something other than wealth is at play.

2. The answer begins with the virtue of generosity. Those at peace with money have one thing in common: over time, they have developed the virtue of generosity.

3. Whether rich or poor, generosity is an issue of the soul, not the pocketbook, so no one is exempt from the struggle. To overcome anxiety about money, one must develop the virtue of generosity.

4. Developing this virtue requires humility, an honest assessment of ourselves, particularly our attachment to material possessions.

5. Unfortunately, self-assessment is not most people's strong suit. God knows this. So in addition to placing an invitation to virtue within our hearts, God also provides grace as a heavenly aid to help us respond.

6. To be generous, then, means to cooperate with God's invitation. In this light, almsgiving, done well, is a distinctly spiritual endeavor.

7. However, for almsgiving to rise to the level of a true spiritual act, two things are necessary. First, free will is essential. If forced in any way — through societal pressure, a manipulated sense of guilt, or the tax code — our giving is not an act of generosity, no matter how noble the ends. Further, spiritual giving requires an attitude that continually turns to God and asks, "What would you have me do with the gifts you have entrusted to me?" Giving — whether time or money — must become a personal response to God's unique invitation to *you*.

It's at this point that worries about money begin to fade. *Having acknowledged the invitation, cooperated with grace, and trusted in his providence, God blesses us with spiritual consolations — not least of which is freedom from persistent worries.*

In a nutshell, that's it. We can all go home. Thanks for coming. Notice the tip jar on your way out.

Is it really that easy?

Yes and no. Concepts are easy. Implementation, growth, conversion — call it what you will — is difficult.

Take, for instance, one small recommendation offered in the last chapter: before judging the worthiness of a charity, we should first allow God to interrogate *us*.

This sounds like simple advice, but implementing it presumes three prerequisites.

- You have a well-formed image and understanding of God.
- You converse with him regularly and have learned to recognize his voice.
- You desire conversion.

That's a tall order. For now, let's focus on just the first point. We have to get that right. It's difficult to hear God's voice if we have a blurred, uncertain, or unapproachable image of him. So before going much further, let's make sure we have the right image of God.

If this sounds too basic, humor me and play along for now. I'd prefer to take nothing for granted. Without jumping to the next paragraph, first answer this question: If most moderns agree that there is one God, why are there so many religions? Pause and reflect on this for a moment: if we all pray to the same God, why isn't there just one religion?

One reason is because the various religions are a reflection of the differing images people have of God. For example, some understand God to be an impersonal judge who demands nothing less than total submission to his will. Others view God as a loving father. Still others believe in a God who created the universe, but who is no longer actively involved in its affairs, like a watchmaker who winds up his invention, then lets it run on its own.

These images are not uncommon, and we don't need to go beyond the bounds of Christianity to find subscribers to each. Even among professed Christians who worship together every Sunday, there are differing images of God that stem from our experience of family, how we were taught, and influences throughout life. We may recite the same Creed, but a deep philosophical discussion with fellow parishioners quickly reveals a ready supply of opinions at odds with each other. Unlike medicine, law, or accounting — where a certain amount of education earns your opinion some credibility — in the realm of theology people oddly assume none is needed. Hence, people cling to a great diversity of images.

To add to the confusion, many people are comfortable with incompatible ideas of God. They don't see a problem if their understanding of God is 180 degrees opposite from the next guy's, as though God has a schizophrenic, dual personality. One has to wonder: Is it possible for God to have so many faces? Is there more than one God? Or is there one true God that's horribly misunderstood by a lot of people?

You can see why I don't want to assume that your image of God is the same as mine. There are many disparate ideas concerning who God *really* is. What assumptions do you make? How do you see God? It's important to have the right image, because I just told you to allow God to interrogate your heart. You don't want the wrong God doing that. You don't want the nasty, mean God on that job. Nor the taskmaster. Nor the disinterested watchmaker. I wouldn't want any of those Gods putting me under the spotlight, and I wouldn't blame you for not wanting it either.

So what understanding of God should we have? Which God should we allow to examine our hearts?

This one:

> [Jesus] said to his disciples, "Therefore I tell you, do not be anxious about your life, what you shall eat, nor about your body, what you shall put on. For life is more than food, and the body more than clothing. Consider the ravens: they neither sow nor reap, they have neither storehouse nor barn, and yet God feeds them. Of how much more value are you than the birds! And which of you by being anxious can add a cubit to his span of life? If then you are not able to do as small a thing as that, why are you anxious about the rest? Consider the lilies, how they grow; they neither toil nor spin; yet I tell you, even Solomon in all his glory was not arrayed like one of these. But if God so clothes the grass which is alive in the field today and tomorrow is thrown into the oven, how much more will he clothe you, O men of little faith! And do not seek what you are to eat and what you are to drink, nor be of anxious mind. For all the nations of the world seek these things; and your Father knows that you need them. Instead, seek

his kingdom, and these things shall be yours as well. (Lk 12:22–31)

When you open your heart to God — asking, "Lord, what would you have me do with my wealth?" — this is the God to have in mind: the one who cares for the lilies of the field. Don't put your trust in any God short of this one.

Trusting an unseen God isn't easy. Every time I attend Mass, I hear the priest pray a beautiful prayer on our behalf. It's short and probably goes mostly unnoticed, but it's a favorite of mine. After we recite the Our Father, and shortly before we receive the Eucharist, the priest prays, "Protect us from all anxiety as we wait in joyful hope for the coming of our Savior, Jesus Christ."[9]

Unfortunately, by the look on people's faces, it's apparent we don't expect him back any time soon. If you've served as a lector and looked out over the congregation, you know what I mean. How many of us live in joyful hope? How is it possible to have a trust so deep that we live our lives, with all its disappointments and troubles, in joyful hope?

It requires the right image of God, one who loves us tenderly and with great compassion. I'm sadly convinced that much of our lives are spent waiting, hoping, yearning to love and be loved with great abandon. There is no greater longing in the contemporary heart than the desire to know true love. Ironically, we wait for love, while God waits for us. It's like we're walking in an orchard filled with delicious fruit, complaining of hunger. All we need do is reach up.

****

I recall with melancholy and fondness the Octobers of my childhood. On the northern prairie, autumn comes much too soon, with little warning and a modicum of mercy. The last vacation days of August could be spent in sweltering 100-degree heat and high humidity. Just six weeks later, residents might awaken to flurries. Somewhere in between, nature gives up the ghost. The shelterbelts of trees that protect the fields from wind erosion all summer suddenly turn golden. Clear, blue skies and calm winds invite the first killing frost, and the next morning the trees seem to know it's "game over."

The beauty rarely lasts more than a day. The inevitable, incessant north wind strips the trees bare, and sends their leaves on a journey south. This is the kind of cold wind that takes the breath away and tears up the eyes. No sense raking leaves in these gray conditions; they're on the move. As a child, I imagined piles of leaves twenty feet deep in South Dakota or Nebraska or wherever the Canadian wind finally blew itself out and dropped its cargo. With a pile like that, you could do a backflip off the garage and not get hurt. Maybe even a swan dive. Watching the leaves head south, I knew that somewhere out there, other kids were having more fun.

In retrospect, I wasn't just feeling left out, I was feeling abandoned. Do geese really need to make such a big show about going south for the winter? For weeks the skies would be filled with their squawking, like relatives shouting good-bye from car windows as they depart down a gravel road. At least the robins and blackbirds just quietly disappeared. They didn't feel a need to stick it in your face.

Still etched in my memory, October's wind made me feel like nature had left us poor humans behind to fend for ourselves. Chasing my baseball hat down the street, I wondered if we were the lowest of creatures, too dim-witted to hibernate or leave. Instead, we humans resigned ourselves to what lay ahead. Each day would grow shorter; each week, colder. The earth around us was dying. Soon the skies would be dark on the way to school.

October is a melancholy month.

But there is fondness in it, too. In 1967, I was in Sister Felicia's second-grade class. Well into her seventies, she was still teaching with the vigor of a woman half her age. She was a member of St. Benedict's order, which was particularly advantageous for her career as an educator: the traditional Benedictine habit and veil added a good four inches to her five-foot frame. The extra height would serve her well when she tangled with certain classmates a second time in junior high.

Founded 1,500 years ago, the Benedictines knew a thing or two about teaching. Imagine, as a child, trying to argue with that kind of history. You don't. Sister Felicia told me to write my last name J-E-F-F-*E-R*-Y rather than J-E-F-F-*R-E*-Y, and I promptly went home to inform my father we had been spelling our name wrong for several generations.

Three days a week we had religion class, and I learned that God made me to know, love, and serve him in this life, and to be happy with him in the next. You have to admire elementary school. They do a good job of packaging the facts. Nice, neat, little bundles that go well with milk.

Wednesdays were special. That was the day Monsignor A. I. Merth would make his rounds of the all the elementary school classes, stopping by to share a greeting and a ten-minute lesson. He was a strong figure, with a handsome face and beautiful white hair. He looked more like a man in his fifties than one who had a right to retire. I didn't know it at the time, but he built the school in which I sat. He was a visionary, a mover and shaker. His holiness, leadership, and long career had earned him the honorary title of monsignor, and the right to wear the cassock with the magenta piping. That just added to the circus excitement as we waited for him to arrive. You would think the pope was coming.

In the background, the radiators clanked, a happy sign that Bill the Janitor had finally got the boilers going against the October cold. From our garden-view classroom we could see the tops of the trucks hauling beets to the nearby plant, where tons of sugar would be refined for tables across America. With the factory less than a mile away, the smell of boiling beets would ride in on the wind, and mix with the scent of summer's dust burning off the radiator. It wasn't incense, but I was warm and safe.

To ready us for Monsignor's visit, Sister had us gather on the floor at the front of the class, a big semicircle of nervous energy. I'm not sure why Monsignor wanted us at his feet. Maybe he was a good politician and liked to "work the crowd," as they say. Mix it up a bit. I prefer to think we were his little sheep and he was our good shepherd.

There we sat in anticipation each Wednesday morning, awaiting Monsignor's arrival. In the meantime, Sister would keep us quiet with stories, which we all enjoyed immensely. I seem to remember tales of butterflies — actually the same story repeated each week — which Sister Felicia improvised with full action. It was about a child in a meadow chasing after a butterfly that refused to be caught. "Reaching, reaching," she would say, as she acted out a child swinging a butterfly net. Despite those multiple performances, I don't recall the end of the story. When Monsignor Merth arrived, the show always abruptly ended. We would stand and greet him, shake out the last bits of restlessness, and sit back down. Monsignor would pull up a chair built for a second grader, lean forward, make the Sign of the Cross, and give his lesson. It was usually a Bible story, or a series of questions that made thirty little arms excitedly arise in unison. Sister Felicia would look on, clearly pleased with her charges, and we knew it.

Monsignor Merth's lessons always ended with an invitation. "Stand and I'll give you my blessing." This was the highlight of the visit, like an extra dollop of ice cream on warm apple pie. Then, with the grace bestowed, he headed straight for the door, but always stopped just short of the exit, in a teasing way as if he had forgotten something. He would turn around and say, "Oh yeah, children. What are you to remember?"

Relief! We knew this one, too. "God loves me," would come the answer in unison. Then, with a smile, he was gone.

******

God loves me.

I wonder if the knocks of life, many of our own making, eventually squeeze this basic truth from our hearts. In its place, all sorts of other images filter in. I will admit I need Monsignor Merth's reminder as much as an adult as I did in second grade. If I'm going to meet God in prayer, if there is to be a heart-to-heart talk, this assurance of love is a baseline prerequisite. Otherwise there's always a bit of fear that keeps me at a distance. I don't think God wants that. He's a merciful God. I know it for a fact.

When I was in sixth grade, my older brother was put in charge of looking after my younger brother and me. John was three years my senior, and usually a good baby-sitter. He went on to become the kind of compassionate, advice-giving brother anyone would be lucky to have. But on one Saturday in 1969 he was feeling particularly squirrely.

I don't remember what he did to get me riled up. It's not like he beat on me. He didn't have to. He was blessed with a verbal proficiency well beyond his years, which he exercised with great dexterity, and I was white-hot with anger. In a flashing instant, I decided it was finally time to stand up for myself. Since I couldn't take him in a fight, I ran to the kitchen and secured a knife. That got his attention.

Since homicide has no statute of limitations, I should make clear that it was a only a butter knife. And I never actually used it. When John saw I was serious, the sport was over, and he decided to leave me alone the rest of the evening.

That solved the immediate problem but created another. I knew our monthly visit to the confessional was just around the corner, and Monsignor Merth or one of his lieutenants would be waiting for me. This little encounter would have to top the list.

When you're a kid, everything seems bigger than it really is. I was nervous, but felt I needed to be courageous. My attitude then, as now, was to always lead with the big sins. Get them right out there. Then taper off slow, hoping by the time the priest heard the last of it, he would have forgotten the big show opener.

No such luck. First there was the pregnant pause. Then from behind the screen I could hear Father sigh. At this point, I just knew this was too much for him. I knew he had never encountered a sinner like me. Finally the questions came: What were the circumstances? How often did this happen? Were my parents carnival workers?

I answered each inquiry honestly but just enough to satisfy the question. No need for unnecessary details. Plus, there was a line outside the confessional door, so maybe could we just get this over?

Then in the nearly total blackness, with only the soft light that filtered through the privacy screen, I could feel the Holy Spirit's presence. Father gave me a bit of advice on dealing with anger and with an older brother, which apparently took, and issued the verdict. For my penance, I was to say three Hail Marys.

Imagine that. "Attempted murder" and I got off with three Hail Marys.

When I speak of a loving, merciful God, this is the one I'm thinking of.

FOR REFLECTION

As this chapter points out, people have a variety of views about God. Some see him as arbitrary, disinterested, judgmental, angry, or worse; all of which are erroneous assumptions.

Having a wrong conception of God stops a lot of people from developing a relationship with him. For many, he's not the kind of person they want around, simply because they fail to see him as Jesus taught us to: as a loving father, full of mercy and compassion, a God who desires only the best for us.

If you want to make peace with money, you have to make peace with God. You will find, as we work our way through the remaining chapters, that the two go hand-in-hand. So now is the time to take stock of how we view God.

1. In one hundred words or less, write out an answer to these questions:
   a. Describe God in your own words. How do you see him?
   b. How do you think God feels about you, personally? Why?
2. Again, for maximum benefit, share what you have written with your money partner, and explain why you wrote what you did.

Chapter 6

Learning to Trust

I said earlier that generosity is the key to making peace with money. To be more exact, the key is trust in a loving God. Generosity is simply evidence of this trust.

As trust in God grows, worries about money lessen, making it easier to be generous with however little or much we have. It would be difficult to develop trust if we thought God was a disinterested, mean-spirited, or demanding master. This is why the previous chapter was so important: we need to have the proper image of God as a kind and merciful father who knows our every need.

I can't emphasize this point enough. It's one thing to say on an intellectual level, "God is love." It's quite another to believe in your gut that God loves you as a distinct individual.

Yet this is the very knowledge needed to be free from persistent worries about money. So this chapter brings us new questions. How is it possible to trust an unseen God? Why do some people feel God's love, while others don't? Why do only some people find their way to faith?

The search for God often begins as an intellectual undertaking. But the trust that overcomes material worries isn't based only in premise and logic. It's a conviction that is felt, and for that we need to pray — another of those easier-said-than-done prescriptions. Even Christians who have been practicing for many years are aware of the battle of prayer, a struggle "against ourselves and against the wiles of the tempter who does all he can to turn man away from prayer, away from union with God."[10]

If experienced Christians can have a hard time with prayer, how much more difficult must it be for individuals who are less sure of a heavenly father? So let's start with this person, the one inclined to say, "I honestly don't know if God really exists. How can I pray to someone when I don't know whether he's even there?" Like millions of people over the centuries, I've asked these questions myself. I know how it feels to want assurance, especially in times of stress. So when I hear comments like these, my heart feels empathy.

My head, however, is less sympathetic. Sincere as these questions may be, I immediately suspect an intellectual shell game because I deceived myself for years asking whether God was real. Rather than just fervently ask him — which now seems like the obvious solution to the question — I spent a lot of time reading psychology, philosophy, and theology. I turned what should be a relationship into an intellectual endeavor.

I finally discovered that intellectual doubt was not the real problem. It was fear. In truth, I instinctively knew God existed, but I didn't want to face him. If we were honest with ourselves, we would admit *this* is what makes prayer difficult for the beginner. We can lie to our boss, put on a good face to our adoring public, and even keep things from our spouse. But God? No chance of pulling one over on him. It seems silly to even try, but that's what humans have attempted since the beginning.

In the Book of Genesis, after Adam ate the forbidden fruit, he knew he was naked. When God came looking for him, he hid. He didn't want to face God for the same reason we don't: fear of being seen for who we truly are. Adam knew he had sinned and didn't want to confront that fact. Neither do we. Professed doubt is usually just intellectual cover, an excuse to avoid getting face-to-face with our Creator.

The fear I'm talking about comes in two forms. The first, just mentioned, is the trepidation of acknowledging our own sinfulness and weakness. This is never a pleasant task. But whom are we kidding? What are we afraid of? Do we really think that God will look at our soul and say with an embarrassed, blushed face, "Well, there's a sin I never expected to see!" Could we be such great sinners as to invent something God hasn't witnessed before, much less forgiven? This is an irrational apprehension, especially in light of God's love and mercy.

I'm very sympathetic to this type of fear. Every time I present myself to God in the sacrament of Reconciliation, I first have to overcome this hesitation. It's one of two tricks the Great Deceiver uses to keep us from turning to God for healing. First, he tries to convince us that our sins really aren't sins at all, or if they are, they're so small they're not worth bothering about — just a little something under the fingernails. If that ploy doesn't work and we still have an inclination to turn back to God, Satan is there with his backup plan the very instant our heart softens. He whispers over our shoulder — quietly as though he were sharing a dark secret — words that convince us that God is not as merciful as we've been led to believe.

Then he instills in us such embarrassment over our misdeeds that we prefer to remain with Adam deep in the woods, running from God. This is a truly wicked scheme meant to keep us separated from God, and I've fallen for it more times than I care to admit.

There is a second fear among those that profess doubt about God's existence, more cunning than the first: many people fear a difinitive answer regarding God's existence. This may seem odd at first glance, but deep down, some people don't really want to know. They fear an answer because settling the question forces a person to accept one of two scenarios.

On the one hand, imagine wholeheartedly pursuing the question only to discover that God is nothing more than wishful thinking. To conclude that God does not exist means the world and your life are simply an accident of nature; there is no ultimate meaning to life or existence after death, only a return to dust. This would be a pretty depressing conclusion for an individual to face.

It's even less appealing for society. To do away with any reference to God in our civic life is to unwittingly sweep away the notion of God-given rights, thus setting the stage for tyranny. Consider Communism. Why did Communist leaders mandate atheism? Why did they feel it necessary to crush any faith in God? Because when citizens felt their government's cruel hand of injustice, they could not argue that their God-given rights had been violated. There was no God! He did not exist. In an officially atheistic society, there are no rights "endowed by our creator" because the government does not acknowledge a creator. Instead, their *leaders* tell the people what rights they have, and what rights they don't have.

Little wonder relatively few people are willing to definitively deny God's existence. We instinctively know that denying God is to deny the notion of God-given rights. Thus, humanity clings to the hope that we are protected by a universal moral authority greater than that claimed by our frail human leaders.

But the other possibility — that God definitively *does* exist — isn't necessarily attractive either. The instant we acknowledge God's presence we suddenly become accountable to him. Think about it. If God exists, we can no longer judge our lives by our own standard or by comparing ourselves with others who seem more sinful than we. To believe what Monsignor Merth taught his second grade class — to believe that "God loves me" — lays waste to the idea that we will decide for ourselves what is right and what is wrong. For Christians, it means now having to judge our lives by God's standard, which is nothing less than the life of Christ. Herein lies the difficulty in acknowledging God's existence. Who wants to be accountable to anyone else, much less God, especially if one mistakenly sees him as something other than a loving father? Ironically, the very thing that could liberate people, and help them find peace, is the thing they often fear most: to acknowledge God means we are no longer our own.

This explains why so many people today prefer to leave the question of God's existence untested. As long as his existence is an open question, we have no other avenue to judge behavior other than our own reason. That, conveniently, can be molded to suit our taste. That's why there's motivation to construct all sorts of intellectual ruses to dismiss the tug we feel on our heart.

This avoidance is not intentional; perhaps we're not even aware of it. Nevertheless, it's there. We happily endorse the modern misconception that it's not possible to know if there is a God, when in fact it is. Thousands of martyrs were so sure of God's existence and his love that they were willing to give their lives in witness to the truth. Certainly, this alone tells us something about whether or not God is knowable.

Yet facts like this are dismissed, and we delay, doing our best to keep belief at bay. When the call on the heart finally becomes so strong that we can no longer deny God's invitation, there is a tendency to take baby steps toward him. The first move is often a vague spirituality, which is very popular these days. We've all known someone who claims to be "spiritual" but doesn't believe in "organized religion."

When I hear such a comment, I have to beat back the temptation to be a smart aleck. "Oh, so you don't believe in organized religion? You should come to my parish. We're anything but organized. We're lucky to pull off a summer picnic!"

I've never used that line, but I'm tempted because I fail to see the benefit of disorganized religion over organized religion. Work with me on this. Imagine someone saying, "I don't believe in organized science." Would you see them as open-minded, or foolish? Imagine the attitude of such a person. "Frankly, I don't feel a need to bow to hundreds of years of scientific thought and discovery. I have my own intellect and can think for myself. Who needs a periodic table of elements? I'll invent my own from scratch."

We would never endorse this sort of attitude. Scientific discoveries are done within the context of a community. Individual research may develop new insights, but the larger scientific community must review the conclusions before they are given acceptance. Why? Part of the reason is that researchers are human. There is a temptation to see in the data only things the researcher wants to see.

The same dynamic is at play in the spiritual life. There is a tendency to notice within ourselves that which we like and to overlook the rest. There is also a tendency to apply this approach to God. We like God's mercy but aren't fond of the whole notion of his justice, particularly when it's applied to us. This is why the spiritual life requires community, that is, "organized" religion. Otherwise the individual can dream up all sorts of notions about God and God's plan for how we ought to live. Conveniently, the God we prefer asks nothing of us. Little wonder many people prefer a custom-made God and a vague spiriuality.

****

Imagine the confidence required to develop one's own religion. For two thousand years some of history's greatest minds have pondered the Scriptures and the life of Christ. Volumes of their writings — peer reviewed and standing the test of time — have been handed down to us from Augustine, Bonaventure, Aquinas, and countless others. Add to this the encyclicals of the Church, themselves the product of a community of believers, that speak to every imaginable human and social situation. Rather than drink from this well, the overly self-confident believe it is better to start from scratch. That's like saying, "Newton, Einstein, Planck? Who needs them?" I'm not sure I could muster the kind of confidence necessary to strike out on my own, and in the process dismiss some two thousand years of lived wisdom.

But many do. Part of what drives people from organized religion is hypocrisy. I'm sympathetic to the charge. I agree that too many of the faithful profess one thing but do another. I've worked in the Church long enough to see some very sad instances of this.

Still, I'd like to put in a good word for hypocrites.

It seems to me there are three types of people. First, there are those who espouse ideals and actually live up to them. For the Christian, this would mean walking perfectly in the steps of Jesus. If this person exists, I haven't met him or her yet.

On the opposite extreme, we have the person who advocates no specific morality. There is no danger of labeling this person a hypocrite. If you have no ideals, you can't be accused of falling short.

Then there are the rest of us, the vast majority who hold certain ideals, even if we come up short now and then. Every time we fail, we open ourselves to the charge of hypocrisy. But what other option is there? I'm not yet perfect, and I suspect it's going to take a while longer to achieve the status of saint, if in fact I ever do. So for now, perfection is off the table.

On the other hand, I could let go of my ideals and convictions. That, too, would save me from the charge of hypocrisy. But if everyone did this, I'm afraid the world would be in a very sorry state, much worse off than it is at present.

Given the options, being a hypocrite — having ideals, but falling short — seems only natural; in fact, the only real choice. The reason that hypocrisy earned such a poor reputation is that certain hypocrites have a blind eye. They espouse ideals, fail to live up to them, and then refuse to see and admit their own shortcomings. This gives all us hypocrites a bad name.

I would argue that it's okay to be a hypocrite, to repeatedly attempt to rise to God's standards, as long as we humbly admit when we fall short. Most people will give this kind of lovable hypocrite a pass; everyone, that is, except the person who espouses no morality whatsoever. The mere suggestion that one ought to live up to certain ideals bugs the daylights out of them.

This sort of person isn't much fun to be around. I'll take a repentant hypocrite any day. That's the guy I want on my team. He's the one that ultimately makes the world a better place, and we need more guys like him. In fact, I was thinking of making up a thousand T-shirts emblazoned with "Hypocrites for Christ." If people understood hypocrisy the way I've just explained it, I think it would be much more fashionable. The concept might even top the platinum-selling "WWJD" — "What would Jesus do?"

****

Studying the "good hypocrite" — the one who espouses ideals, falls short, repents, and tries again — can be very helpful to our purposes because in this person we see the process of conversion. To learn to trust God requires conversion, and it's usually a long drawn-out affair, with two steps forward and one step back. But every now and then God grows tired of our whining, and sends forth an extra helping of grace to get us over a particularly devilish hump. For these occasions, he has given us Irish priests, who are in a category unto themselves. There is a salt-of-the-earth quality to the Irish that makes their priests much beloved by penitents. If you want mercy without a lot of pie-in-the-sky philosophizing, an Irish priest is your best bet.

Knowing this, I wasn't prepared for the question posed to me several summers ago. Rather than try to make the fifteen minutes set aside for confessions before daily Mass, which lends itself to a "just the facts, ma'am" form of the sacrament, I took advantage of the Saturday afternoon full-hour time slot. This was always dangerous, especially if the day was bright and sunny and few "customers" showed up. In these circumstances the priest may feel free to take his time and initiate a little chat to get to the bottom of things.

Such was the case on that Saturday afternoon. I arrived to find just two other penitents, both white-haired little grandmas with walkers. As I took my place in line, I wondered, "What could they possibly have to confess?" Then I thought of the grocery store check-out, and began to worry that I had inadvertently followed these ladies into the "seven items or less" line.

Instead of daydreaming, I should have been praying. Suddenly I was alone in line, next up to bat. It was hard to pray, because I kept wondering what the priest was thinking, sitting in the confessional on a sunny Saturday afternoon, waiting for the last in line to enter. I just imagined him saying to himself, "There's no one else here. We have all the time in the world. Why not have a really good soul washing with this last lad?"

The more I thought about it, the more nervous I became at the possibility of a spiritual workout. Then an idea struck me. Why not ask the Holy Spirit to intervene? It just might work. Plus, I was out of time. As Grandma #2 left the confessional, I whispered a prayer to the Holy Spirit. "You do the talking."

That was all the invitation God needed.

In keeping with my aforementioned policy, I led with the first-class sins, with some of my favorites. But this time, as I heard my own words, I felt the weight of their ugliness. This was not a game. I had really offended God, who deserved all my love.

Though I had chosen to kneel behind the privacy screen, rather than sit across from Father O'Hara, my voice betrayed what I was feeling. With great compassion, he asked me, "Do you want to be free of your sin?"

The question caught me off-guard. I quickly responded with a curt, "Yes, Father." He went on to share some advice, assign a penance, and grant absolution, but I honestly heard none of it. I was still stuck on the question. Did I really want to be free of my sin?

As I returned to the pew, I realized that I had just lied to a priest, in the confessional no less. I didn't want to be free of my sin. Maybe at this moment I did, but I knew from experience it wouldn't last for long. That's why I had returned over and over with the same sins.

This set me on a path to realize that every sin is like the sweet-sour jawbreakers I used to eat as a kid. The outside is covered with pure sugar, colored and pretty. I always loved that part, until the sugar melted away and I was left with the sour center. Every sin is like that jawbreaker. There is always something initially attractive that later gives way to emptiness, disappointment, and a bad taste in the mouth. Why do people gossip? Because it feels good to be in the know — until no one dares befriend the person for fear of lost confidence. Why do people swear and allow themselves fits of rage? Because it feels good to let off steam at any cost — until loved ones are permanently pushed away. Why are there gluttons? Because eating is enjoyable — until diabetes forces trips to the doctor and daily blood tests.

Every sin holds an empty promise. Little wonder the Church speaks of the glamour of evil. That's the perfect word. Going back more than three centuries, the word "glamour" may have implied defective sight, like one who suffers from glaucoma. Later, it would come to be associated with learning in the occult arts. By 1913, *Webster's* first of four definitions described glamour as "a charm affecting the eye, making objects appear different from what they really are."[11] As commonly used today, glamorous is often taken to mean simply "attractive," rather than the more accurate, "deceptively attractive." We seem to have forgotten the part of the definition that tells us we've been hoodwinked.

But the Church has not forgotten. In the baptismal rites for adults, the priest asks the catechumen, "Do you reject the glamour of evil, and refuse to be mastered by sin?"[12]

The question itself speaks volumes about human nature. It acknowledges that evil has certain attractive qualities; it is glamorous, and it beckons to us. But rather than ask the soon-to-be-baptized person to make a pledge to never sin again, it asks whether the person refuses "to be mastered by sin." This is nothing short of brilliant. The Church knows human weakness, so instead the question merely asks whether the individual is ready to engage in the struggle. That's all the Church asks. Are you ready to do battle? Do you promise to not give in? When you fall, do you promise to come back swinging?

This should be the great consolation of all sinners, to know that God simply asks that we stay in the fight and strive for holiness. To give up the struggle means to be "mastered by sin." And if sin becomes the master, consider who the slave might be.

FOR REFLECTION

There is a difference between *assuming* something is true, and *knowing* it's true. Some people have been church-goers all their lives, but have never stopped to consider whether they are certain God exists and loves them. This is critical, because only a deep trust in God can ultimately tame persistent worries about money.

If this describes your circumstance, may I suggest a path forward?

At this very moment, all you need do is pray this simple prayer: "Heavenly Father, please reveal yourself to me. I want to accept all the graces you have in store for me."

It's really that simple. You don't need a lot of words, just a sincere heart, persistence, and patience. It may take minutes, days, or months before the prayer is answered. But it will be answered, in God's own way. Sometimes he needs a bit of "lead time" to prepare hearts. Again, be persistent in asking. We have a generous God, and he will answer you. That reply may come in one of two ways.

1. It is possible to reason our way to God's existence using our own intellect. Philosophers and saints have trod this path for centuries. In praying for God's assistance, he may lead you toward opportunities to enlighten your intellect through reading or conversations with others.

2. God can grant the favor of infused knowledge, a conviction he himself plants directly in the soul. This is an inexplicable knowledge, an extraordinary gift. Suddenly, you "just know."

Either way, when God answers your prayer, don't forget to say thanks.

Chapter 7

Notes on Conversion

You may have purchased this book hoping for financial advice and instead — by design — I've led you on a journey inward. Financial freedom is not found in any amount of money, but in the trust one has in God's providence. *It's impossible to make peace with money until you make peace with God.* This is the real solution to the ailment.

So rather than focus on just one aspect of growth — generosity — let us go further. It wouldn't make sense to bus the dishes from the table, only to leave the sink full of dirty pots and pans. If you're going to clean the kitchen, you might as well do the whole thing and enjoy the result. That's my attitude. As long as we've come this far, why not open our entire lives to God? There is no reason to be put off by this. There is nothing to fear. God is going to take care of you, financially and otherwise; and the more you come to know him, the more assured you will be of this fact.

So let's return to the notion of conversion introduced in the last chapter. It's a simple idea. It means turning back toward God. When you think of conversion, it should feel like going home to the place you always wished you had.

Not too many people see it this way, probably because we remember friends in college who complained about a common acquaintance, as in, "Julie used to be a lot of fun, until she had her *conversion*." Of course, the word would be drawn out with a thinly veiled disgust ("con-VERRRRR-sion") as though little Miss Julie had stepped in something quite unpleasant. Implied, if not stated, was the corollary that she had, in the process, ceded her intellect to the Thought Police, most likely because she couldn't handle the real world.

What arrogant nonsense. In reality, conversion is about engaging the real world, starting with ourselves and our shortcomings. It is going to a place where you will be loved for who you are, and not for what you have. To say "I want conversion" is to say, "I don't want to live this way any more. I want something better."

At the moment, maybe "something better" means a lifting of anxiety about your financial future. Or, to my earlier point, something better might be more comprehensive. It could also be a desire to be free of those sins that keep you in a rut, the ones you've grown so accustomed to that you hardly notice them any more. Maybe you have given up trying, despondent that you'll ever conquer them.

If so, it's important to remember that all sin, even the silly little sins of childhood, add a weight to the soul. This is not metaphor. It is a weight that can actually be felt. It is called acedia, "a form of depression due to lax ascetical practice, decreasing vigilance, carelessness of heart."[13]

As I ride the subway I often wonder how many Americans suffer from acedia, a gray cloud that "goes so far as to refuse the joy that comes from God."[14] I have my suspicions, because there are an awful lot of long faces. Maybe the whole carload just had a trying day at the office. Or maybe I'm looking at a hundred commuters, each wondering which frozen dinner to pop in the microwave. That's possible. It could be they're just hungry. Or lonely. Big cities are very lonely places. A farmer friend recently visited from Wisconsin, and over beer he commented that he had never seen such a lonely place as Washington, D.C. "They don't talk to each other!" he observed of riders on the Metro. I had to agree with him. Until I grew accustomed to the social conventions, it seemed peculiar to press in so close to strangers and not venture eye contact or a greeting, especially with such a tired, hungry, lonely bunch of folks.

Or maybe it really is acedia. I'll let God be the judge. I'm just stating the facts, and my friend from Wisconsin will back me up: most people just don't look happy. I try to convince myself it's none of my business, but I can't help wonder how many have ever experienced the joy of conversion, of heading home to God, turning around and saying to him, "I missed you." Who wouldn't want this? The thought that millions of people may be missing out on the fullness of life burdens me greatly.

But at least we have each other. So let's begin, again. That's what conversion is all about, choosing to start over.

We'll start with a short exercise. Imagine yourself standing behind me in the confessional line, waiting and preparing for a little chat with Father O'Hara. Quick — without too much thought — what's the first thing that comes to mind, the first indiscretion you would get off your chest? Gluttony, envy, impatience, lust, lies, gossip, indifference: these are just some of the maladies we mortals face. Of all the possibilities, one will come to mind first. If not, ask the Holy Spirit for help. Ask God to allow you to see your soul as he sees it. When you sincerely offer this simple prayer, chances are good you will feel an immediate pinprick in your heart. If so, you are lucky. You have just been graced by God. Don't fight it. Accept it. There will be a temptation to dismiss the discomfort, but the uneasiness is part of the grace.

Now ask yourself, "Do I want to be free of this sin?" Here's where honesty is crucial. You may discover, as I did, that you quite enjoy sin, even though you feel it is holding you back from something better.

Remember that every sin comes wrapped in a deceptive sweetness. To simply attack your favorite sin with brute willpower is usually an exercise in futility. Not that firm conviction isn't a good idea — it is, and it's necessary. I just know how the Devil works. He teases the repentant mind with an extra tablespoon of sugar heaped upon the sin, to make it look doubly delicious once you begin to miss it. And you will miss it. After all, we're talking about your favorite sin, which over the years may have grown to resemble a comforting friend.

Here's where we need to fight fire with fire.

Rather than a vague prayer for help, ask God to take away the pleasure you find in the sin. How's that for cunning? It's very effective, but you may find it's not an easy request to make. Most of us are like St. Augustine of Hippo, the fourth-century north African bishop whose conversion was delayed by faddish spiritual curiosities and youthful indiscretion. To paraphrase the angelic doctor, "Please help me Lord, just not yet."

When we ask God to take away the pleasure we find in our favorite sin, it gives him permission to do something specific that we can notice. Take gluttony for example. With two-thirds of Americans overweight to one degree or another, it's probably safe to assume that at least a few of us are indebted to this sin. If you are among them, try this: ask God to take away the inordinate pleasure you find in overeating. You will still enjoy food, maybe even more so. But if you sincerely, regularly pray this prayer, you will find that the moment consumption crosses from nourishment to excess, God will let you know. He's there for you. He has your back. One forkful will be delicious, the next less so. At this point, cooperate with grace, quickly, before the Tempter intervenes to ruin a good thing.

Over time, you will come to have an aversion to that stuffed, sleepy feeling that used to give comfort. It won't feel good anymore, and long before you reach this point you will notice grace working here, withdrawing pleasure from the act of eating once you've had enough.

Of course, this occurs naturally. The last bite of pie is never as good as the first. But with grace, this natural phenomenon becomes more pronounced and noticeable. This is what is meant when theologians say grace builds on nature.

Gluttony is just one example. The same principle works for any of the sins listed above. Pray to God to take away the pleasure in the sin, be consistent in prayer, and sincerely give God permission to do what you are asking him to do.

There is another way to move toward God. Ask him to teach you the joy of following his ways. This is an age-old approach found in the psalms. "Behold, you desire truth in the inward being; therefore teach me wisdom in my secret heart" (Ps 51:6). The psalmist goes on to sing, "Make me hear joy and gladness; let the bones which you have broken rejoice" (Ps 51:8).

The idea here is to trade pleasure, which is temporary and fleeting, for joy, which is deeper, more fulfilling, and resilient. The following analogy may limp a bit, but it's the difference between a bowl of ice cream and rock hard abs. The first is pleasurable to be sure, but fleeting. When the ice cream is gone, you don't necessarily feel any better than before you indulged, and in fact, you may even feel worse. The pleasure lasts only as long as the ice cream.

In contrast, a healthy body is with you twenty-four hours a day. It feels good to be fit, and the satisfaction spills over into every other facet of life.

This notion of trading pleasure for joy works particularly well for almsgiving. Money can provide a certain amount of personal pleasure, and that can be a good thing. But the pleasure that comes from spending money is different than the joy of giving it away. In the first case, we benefit ourselves, and so feel an immediate gratification. In the second, there is the satisfaction of helping another person. This tends toward joy, lasts longer, and is generally more resilient. By this I mean that a particular purchase for ourselves may initially delight the senses, but soon fades to just another item among many possessions. But to help another person — to provide food, clothing, shelter, education — is a joy that lingers.

Even so, to say that joy is more satisfying than short-term pleasure does not make almsgiving, or any other good act, immediately easy. It will always be a struggle. This is why I'm lucky to have Stella for a wife. She understands this.

Before we were married we attended the Church-mandated preparation classes, which included a compatibility survey designed to ensure that soon-to-be-married couples have discussed all the big issues that can later haunt a marriage. The survey came back with green lights in all categories except finance. We needed to talk more about money.

Boy, did we. In the first month after we were married, Stella agreed to take on the responsibility of paying bills, and I would balance the checkbook. This way, we would both have a feel for our financial situation. But at month's end, when I saw how much she had given to charity, I nearly had a heart attack. Did she intend such generosity or was this a mistake?

Stella explained that she had recently been making $19,000 a year as a youth minister, and happily giving away about $3,000. This explained why, when I met her, she was rooming in a garage-turned-low-scale-apartment and sleeping on the floor. Here, finally, was the back story to what I thought was just a funky Bohemian lifestyle.

The early days of marriage are filled with all sorts of assumptions, and she assumed that since I made a living asking other people to be generous, I would meet that standard myself. Of course, in my eyes, I was. Like most Catholics, I was giving between 1 and 2 percent, and feeling very good about it. Stella took the concept of tithing literally. To her it meant 10 percent off the top, the first fruits. I thought she was crazy. "No one gives away that kind of money," I incorrectly argued with her.

In retrospect, I shouldn't have balked. Compared to taxes, 10 percent makes God look frugal. What was there to complain about? But this was at a time in my life when I didn't distinguish between taxes and true charity.

I looked calmly into Stella's baby-blue eyes. "We need to talk about this." She gave me that compassionate, patient look wives use when they know they are certain to eventually win an argument. "How much would you like to give?" she asked.

"How about 2 percent?" I suggested. "How about 5?" she quickly countered, as though she was selling cattle at auction.

We settled on 3 percent, which made me feel pretty good. Certainly, winning a debate this early in the marriage would set the right tone for the future. In reality, I was walking in the ranks of naïve young husbands who hadn't yet become familiar with the phrase "steel sharpens steel." But I was about to learn.

When we upped the giving to 3 percent and were still able to pay the bills, Stella suggested we move to 4 percent. When that proved possible, she suggested 5. Then 6. Paradoxically, as the amount increased, each step grew easier. I still was inclined to drag my feet, and complain a bit, but there was a growing conviction that Stella was right.

Finally, somewhere in the fifth year of marriage, I gave Stella the checkbook and told her to take us all the way to a true tithe of 10 percent. She didn't even have to ask. I just offered. Even at this point, however, it felt a bit like giving blood. That too, is a good thing to do, but as the sleeve is rolled up, and the needle inserted, there is a tendency to want to look the other way. That's why I gave Stella the checkbook. "Just do it," I told her.

From this point onward I found myself worrying less and less about money. At the same time, the phone rang with more and more business. Then the dot-com bubble burst, soon followed by the attacks of September 11, 2001. Suddenly the economy wasn't doing so well, and — financially — neither were we.

Despite the situation, Stella and I chose to attend a fund-raising banquet, an event that had become an annual commitment on our calendar. As expected, after dinner the pledge cards were distributed around the table. We had been loyal supporters of this charity for at least five years, but when I looked at the pledge card, I assumed this year's commitment would be different. Ten percent of nothing is nothing. I whispered to Stella, "How much do you want to give?"

She gave me a blank "what a silly question" look. "Do your normal," she said flatly.

I reminded her that I had just deposited the last check from my current client, the contract was completed, and I had no work booked for the foreseeable future. I didn't even have any prospects on the line.

"That's okay," she said calmly.

Obviously, she knew what she was doing. So I made the same twelve-month commitment as the previous year, signed my name, and turned in the pledge. Then a most amazing thing happened. When we got home, there was a message on our voicemail. At the very moment I was signing the pledge, a pastor whom I had previously served was — completely unknown to me — pitching my services to the finance council of another parish. He had even brought along a couple of trustees to make the case, just for good measure. He called to say he had all but closed the deal for me. Within a week I went to work for a new client.

If this were an isolated case, I would attribute it to mere coincidence. But over the last decade I've seen enough examples to conclude that God really does keep his promises to us little sparrows.

There's a lot to be learned here. First, trusting God takes time. For me, it was about a five-year process. Second, conversion often amounts to a series of decisions. I first learned to trust God with 3 percent of my income, then 4, 5, and 6. In a sense, without realizing what I was doing, I was putting God to the test, which in any other realm of life is considered a no-no. But in almsgiving, God invites it. "Bring the full tithes into the storehouse, that there may be food in my house; and thereby put me to the test, says the Lord of hosts, if I will not open the windows of heaven for you and pour down for you an overflowing blessing" (Mal 3:10).

This is exactly what happened. With each step I took, God proved he would look after Stella and me, until I was finally ready for the big test at the fund-raising banquet.

Up until that time I spent considerable effort trying to understand the ways of God, hoping an intellectual approach would advance my faith. Little did I know that one thousand years earlier St. Anselm coined a phrase, probably for skeptics just like me: "I believe that I may understand." He held that reason can help explain faith, but often faith precedes understanding. Faith comes first; then things begin to make sense in life. In this case, it was only when I believed God's promise, beautifully made in the Book of Malachi, and acted upon it, that I understood the futility of worry about money.

Looking back, I can track how my almsgiving eventually matured from burdensome to playful. A few years after the banquet, Stella and I had a particularly good year and wanted to do something special for charity. I learned about a planned gift called a deferred gift annuity. The concept was simple. We made a lump-sum gift to a charity which they invested. The gift grows for twenty-five years, and when I retire the charity will begin making modest payments to us until we die. At that point, whatever is left in the annuity account will be used by the charity in keeping with our stated intentions.

It's actually a very common gift, and if invested well, can grow quite handsomely over a twenty-five-year period. On average, after accounting for payments to the beneficiary of the annuity, about half the ultimate pool of money ends up going to the charity.

The fun part about making the gift was deciding how we wanted the charity to use it. We actually ended up making two gifts, his and hers, so that we could each decide exactly how we wanted our money used. Stella was much more creative.

A few years earlier, she had received a call from Bishop James Sullivan of the Diocese of Fargo, with an invitation to apply for a job. We were living in Ohio at the time and hoping to return to North Dakota, so the call was appreciated. We flew to Fargo and had an opportunity to meet with the bishop as a couple. At the end of a very cordial visit, I asked Bishop Sullivan, "What's the number one thing you want to see happen in your diocese?" Without a word, he poked his finger into my belly, as though I were the Pillsbury Dough Boy. Not sure what the poke was all about, I felt an awkward silence rise up within me. Finally, he looked me square in the eye, "Get out and ring door bells."

Here was a man who wasn't content to complain about the deterioration of the culture. He wanted those who professed to be Christian to do something about it. We had Good News, and he wanted it spread the way it had been done since the time of St. Paul, person-to-person, one-on-one, soul-by-painstaking-soul.

Stella remembered this encounter, and when it came time for her to decide to whom she wanted to give her deferred gift annuity, she chose the Fargo Diocese. Hopefully, she will live another thirty or forty years, we'll receive a little support during our retirement, and the gift will grow to a meaningful sum. Then, when we both die, the assets of the fund will finally be freed for use by the diocese. Here's where the fun begins. I like to imagine the look on the face of some future development officer when he opens a dusty file to read the restrictions Stella placed on the gift.

1. The diocese is free to give the fund to any parish in the diocese that asks for it.

2. The parish can use the money for anything it wants.

3. There is one small stipulation to receive the money, however. The parish needs to make best efforts for a three-year period to visit every household within its parish boundaries.

In short, Stella wants to see Bishop Sullivan's doorbell-ringing vision realized. I wonder whether there will be any takers on the offer. I can just imagine a pastor many years from now declaring to his cash-strapped finance council, "Folks, I have some good news, and some bad news."

Too bad I'll be dead. I'd love to see their reaction.

FOR REFLECTION

Think of your "favorite" sin, the one that's your Achilles' heel. If you are Catholic, it's easy to identify because it's the one that you continually bring back to the Sacrament of Reconciliation.

1. In a short paragraph, answer these questions:

   a. How long have you been doing battle with this weakness? What about this sin keeps you chained to it?

   b. Have you ever considered whether you truly want to be free from this sin?

   c. What has stopped you from asking God for help? Have you considered asking God to take away the "pleasure" you find in your sin? If not, why not?

2. Write out your answers in private. Even though your words are intended for no one but yourself and God, the act of writing is part of bringing your sinfulness into the light, an important first step toward victory.

Chapter 8

Three Temptations against Generosity

If you have come this far in an effort to overcome worries about money, you are ready to tackle the steepest part of the climb. And, like any journey, a guide is helpful; he brings our attention to interesting points that would otherwise go unnoticed, and cautions us regarding things of which we should be wary. In this chapter, we explore the changes in our *external actions* that are needed if we are to trust in God and grow in virtue. In the next, we search the *interior life* for clues that *motivate* our behavior. For this endeavor, we'll need a proven guide.

St. John of the Cross, a Doctor of the Church who lived during the time of the Reformation, is known as one of the great mystics in Spanish literature. He wrote about the journey of the soul to God and the stumbling blocks along the way. His work has been studied for centuries, but for our purposes it is enough to capture an overarching idea in his writings. St. John understood that the path to conversion brings the soul through two periods he called "dark nights."

The first is the "dark night of the senses," in which the soul awakens to the reality of sin. In this period of the spiritual life, the scales of self-deception fall from our eyes, and we begin to see ourselves for who we are — sinners in need of redemption.

This awakening initiates a resolute battle with sin. Feeling the weight of our transgressions, there are attempts at change, but too often only limited success. The soul is spiritually immature, still relying primarily on human powers of intellect and will in its attempts to extinguish sin. Thus, the spiritual life at this point feels as though the soul is grasping in vain toward heaven. With mixed results in the pursuit of holiness, this is a painful time in life that proves very humbling.

Still, progress will be made because now there is a much truer self-knowledge. But even though certain negative behaviors might be extinguished, the soul is far from attaining perfection. For that, St. John of the Cross describes a second period, "the dark night of the soul," in which the interior imperfections that animate sin are finally dealt with directly by God. Realizing the inability to attain perfection on one's own, the penitent is left with no option other than to make best use of his own powers while "waiting on the Lord." Then, at a time appointed by God, grace is infused directly into the soul. This is a new and exhilarating experience. Rather than feeling as though one is reaching up toward God, the penitent is now aware that God is graciously reaching down toward him. That's a profound difference.

St. John of the Cross intended the two "dark nights" as imagery applicable to the whole of one's spiritual life. But for our purposes the metaphor is easier to understand if we look at the example of a single failing and follow the path toward God and redemption. From there, we will apply what we learn to the many issues surrounding generosity, greed, mercy, and envy. They are all areas that must be addressed more deeply if we are to overcome anxieties about money.

When Stella and I got married, she found it puzzling that we received so many clocks as gifts. She didn't understand that the clocks were an inside joke from my extended family, who knew I was notorious for being late.

I soon discovered that tardiness would not fly as a married man. To apply St. John's metaphor, this was a first "dark night": a startled recognition of yet another area of self-centeredness. I had to face the fact that making others wait is rude. Humbly admitting my failing, I set about the painful process of changing my behavior.

However, this first step — extinguishing exterior behaviors — was not enough. A second, deeper conversion, more difficult than the first still lay before me. Eventually I would need to deal with the interior imperfections that gave me quiet permission to be late. I had to rid myself of an arrogant attitude that led me to believe my time was more valuable than others. A second dark night would be needed to conquer this failing: I had to give God permission to work with the underlying selfishness that motivated my tardiness.

This simple example illustrates the key insight of St. John of the Cross: full conversion entails two dark nights, two periods of change. The first is an effort we make to change our behavior, all the while asking God's help. The second is an abundant outpouring of grace, an answer to prayer, in which God seeks to not only change the behavior, but heal the interior attitudes that animate sin.

As we saw in the example above, St. John's overarching notion of two dark nights, though intended as a metaphor for the entire spiritual life, can be applied to those working to deal with any sin or weakness. In our present endeavor, it will be helpful as we strive to attain perfection in generosity.

That's a tall order. In this chapter we deal with the struggle to first change *external* behavior. To use St. John's metaphor, we'll engage at the level of the "dark night of the senses." In the next chapter, we'll examine generosity at a deeper level — "the dark night of the soul" — where we find the *interior* battle between mercy and envy.

Changing behavior is never easy. Even St. Paul acknowledged, "I do not understand my own actions. For I do not do what I want, but I do the very thing I hate" (Rom 7:15). He went on to admit, "I can will what is right, but I cannot do it" (Rom 7:18). With these words, we have arrived at the steepest part of the climb.

We will apply ourselves to the virtue of generosity in a moment. But first, let's look at change in general. Let's break it down, step by step. How does change — conversion — happen? What are the stumbling blocks?

Imagine making a resolution to lose weight. It might go quite well for a day or two, or even a week. At some point, however, the intellect begins to justify the forbidden behavior. Intellect is the ability to reason, and it does a good job providing logical grounds to do what we want. "I've been good all week," the intellect says to justify something sweet. "Just one cookie won't hurt." Then emotion adds its silent voice, with the stress and disappointments of the week welling up in the heart. Given this twin assault, the will — the keeper of the keys, so to speak — relents and the hand reaches for the cookie jar.

In short, there is thought, feeling, and action, an interplay of intellect, emotion, and will.

Of the three, our thought — the intellect — almost always precedes the justification of an action. Put simply, thought precedes action. Another example: perhaps you're familiar with a sign seen frequently in big cities, "Don't even THINK of parking here!" The owner of the sign knows that before a person parks a car in his private spot, the driver must ask himself or herself, "I wonder if I can just sneak in here?" The sign nips that idea in the bud.

Applying this principle to the dieter, once the legs lift the body toward the kitchen and the cookie jar, the battle for virtuous restraint is most likely lost. Resistance is much more effective if engaged with prayer at the first signs of temptation, at the initial thoughts that will eventually lead to the cookie jar.

Jesus alludes to this aspect of human nature when he says, "You have heard that it was said, 'You shall not commit adultery.' But I say to you that every one who looks at a woman lustfully has already committed adultery with her in his heart" (Mt 5:27–28). Of course, there is no sin in being tempted. The problem begins when we *entertain* and *enjoy* the thought of acting on the temptation. That's where temptation crosses the line into sinful thought, and eventually into sinful action. Here is the brilliance of Jesus' teaching. In this passage, he points out that the problem begins long before the act; it originates in the mind, with the power of the intellect to imagine what could be. Because thought precedes action, the time to do battle is at the first sign of temptation.

We are finally ready to apply these principles and insights to the virtue of generosity. If we are to change external behavior, we must be aware of the thought-precedes-action principle. In this case, the "thoughts" are three common temptations against generosity. If these thoughts are entertained for any length of time, they take hold of the soul and silently thwart efforts to change.

If you are serious about growing in virtue, put these three temptations on your "watch list" to avoid falling into their trap:

Temptation 1. "I don't make enough to give anything to charity."

Most people are familiar with the story of the widow's mite, since it appears in both the Gospels of Mark and Luke.

> And he sat down opposite the treasury, and watched the multitude putting money into the treasury. Many rich people put in large sums. And a poor widow came, and put in two copper coins, which make a penny. And he called his disciples to him, and said to them, "Truly, I say to you, this poor widow has put in more than all those who are contributing to the treasury. For they all contributed out of their abundance; but she out of her poverty has put in everything she had, her whole living." (Mk 12:41–44)

One of the amazing things about Scripture is the amount that is said and taught with so few words. This paragraph is a prime example. First, we are told that Jesus "sat down opposite the treasury, and watched the multitude." This alone says something: Jesus didn't just happen to wander by and see the widow making her gift. He "sat down opposite the treasury," as if to purposefully study human behavior. Further, since he watched "the multitude" make their gifts, he must have been there awhile. Apparently, Jesus had an interest in money, but it wasn't in whether the temple raised enough to meet its expenses. His concern centered on the donor, and what was happening in the heart of the person contributing to the treasury.

Given Jesus' interest, the logical conclusion is that almsgiving should also be a concern for today's priests and ministers. Unfortunately, many completely sidestep the topic, reluctant to broach the subject from the pulpit for fear of hearing, "All the pastor ever talks about is money!" I've worked for scores of priests over the years to help parishes organize capital campaigns to repair churches or add facilities. With great pride, many told me when we first met, "I've never once asked my parishioners for money." The assumption embedded in this statement is as silly as it is common: because their parishioners have never been asked, they will have no excuse to refuse a request; the sheer rarity of being asked will yield an outpouring of goodwill and money.

It's simply not true. To make a point, I share with those pastors a parable of my own. "Imagine a mother with a young boy. For seventeen years she never once asks him to make his bed or clean his room, thinking it better to wait until he turns eighteen. Of course, because she has never asked, when she finally does, her son will immediately have the room tidy and clean from that point on. *He'll be the perfect little housekeeper because he has never been asked to do it."*

The illogic of the punch line usually elicits a sheepish laugh from the pastor. How often must a mother tell her young son to pick up his room before he develops the virtue necessary to make it a habit? Point made: the flock learns generosity when the pastor teaches generosity, and it takes time.

Priest and ministers would advance the spiritual life of their parishioners if they spoke more about giving and its spiritual aspects long before money was needed. But too often they are reluctant because they themselves don't understand the spiritual aspects of almsgiving, or perhaps find it hard to articulate. So they only speak of money when absolutely necessary, and give in to the temptation to justify the request for funds on a transactional basis ("Look at all the good the Church does; clearly we are a deserving charity") or guilt ("Your grandparents built this ornate church when they were still living in sod houses, certainly you can do your part today!").

Jesus clearly had an interest in the heart of the donor and the act of selfless generosity. Unfortunately, pastors' reluctance to talk about tithing leaves their parishioners like the eighteen-year-old boy who was never asked to clean his room. We don't know how to give because we have never been taught.

In this light, our culpability is lessened, which may give you some comfort — especially as it pertains to a second lesson quietly nestled within the parable of the widow's mite. Notice what Jesus did not do. When he saw the widow pull two coins from her purse, he didn't run over to her, urging caution. He didn't say, "Excuse me, ma'am. What are you doing? I hope you're not thinking of putting your last two coins in the treasury! What will you eat tonight?"

In fact, he did the opposite. He called together his disciples and endorsed her behavior, which tells us that even the widow was called to generosity. Most homilists miss this point, preferring to spin the story into an accusation that those who "put in large sums" did not put in enough. Focusing on the amount, large or small, misses the point of the story altogether: *Jesus is not concerned with how much people give to God, only how much they trust in God.* The gift is a reflection of trust. In making her gift, the widow was trusting in God's providence completely, while the rich had enough in reserve to still rely on their own wherewithal.

So be aware if you find yourself thinking, "I don't have it to give." If you examine your heart, and are honest with yourself, you may find it's more accurate to recast this statement as, "Since I have little, if I give even a small portion I will have to rely even more on the Lord. I don't think I want to do that."

I realize this statement sounds harsh, but Jesus had every opportunity to explain to his disciples that the widow, in her poverty, did not need to contribute. Instead, he chose to praise her, which tells me it's a behavior he sought to encourage — even for those who claim "I don't make enough to give anything to charity."

Temptation 2. "I already give more than others."

It used to be common practice in Catholic parishes to list the donations of each registered family in an annual report. This unfortunate custom was an indication of the lack of understanding that most pastors had concerning almsgiving. Rather than lift up parishioners' hearts and minds to the spiritual consolations God infuses into the generous heart, pastors relied on social pressure and guilt to ensure the parish met budget.

Not only was this practice devoid of spiritual benefit, it had the potential to backfire. Just a few years ago I came across a rural parish who still published the amount each household had donated for the year. The pastor complained to me that he was unable to meet mounting bills and showed me the annual donations report in the hope that I could offer some advice.

"Here's your problem, Father," I quickly observed. "Your top donor gave just $300 for the year, and everyone now knows it." Complicating the situation, the top donor farmed fifteen thousand prime acres and everyone knew that, too. This family had inadvertently set a benchmark for the rest, and it wasn't much of a high jump. The problem was obvious: people didn't give from a spiritual perspective. Rather, they looked at what their neighbors gave and justified their own poor response in comparison to others.

Thankfully, the practice of publishing donor amounts is extremely rare today. Still, it's not uncommon to see parish annual reports that aggregate data and show the number of families who give $5,000 or more, $3,000-$4,999, and so on, right down to the number of nondonors. These reports, while protecting the privacy of the individual, provide a certain level of transparency concerning gift revenue, and illustrate for parishioners the importance of significant giving to the overall financial health of a parish. So they do serve some purpose. Unfortunately, even aggregated data can be used by families to compare themselves with others.

If you are among this group — with a tendency to think, "I already give more than others" — nip Temptation 2 in the bud because it will stop you from growing in virtue. Your generosity, rightly understood, has nothing to do with the amount your neighbor gives. It's between you and God. If someone else is taking and not giving, it is simply a sign that their spiritual life has not yet matured to a point where they are ready to trust God. We all come from that same place, so have patience. Focus on your own level of trust and your own giving. Enjoy how good it feels to be able to share in God's work.

Temptation 3. "Why should I give more when others give nothing?"

This thought, if entertained for any length of time, is sure to set back the individual striving to develop the virtue of generosity. It's similar to the question previously considered, only more virulent because it is accompanied with a sense of injustice that leads to stern judgment. I've often heard committee members remark about their fellow parishioners, "They could give *something*!"

When we support a common cause like a parish, and discover that others who share in the benefit give nothing, the first reaction is a sense of injustice. But this response is just a sign that we've fallen back into the notion that our gifts are a transaction, a quid pro quo. It's as though we are saying, "I paid for XYZ service, and others should, too."

While it's true that all parishioners have a moral obligation to support the parish, others' nonperformance doesn't justify ours. As my mother used to say, "Two wrongs don't make a right." God has yet to deal with the nondonors, and he will in his own time. Focus, instead, on your own circumstance and attitudes. As we saw in chapter 4, gifts to charity are not a purchase. When we give to a parish, we are not renting a seat in the pew, guaranteeing a lovely spot for our daughter's wedding, or "paying our share of the tab" as I've heard some people remark. To see giving as a transaction turns almsgiving into just another purchase. That is particularly harmful to our spiritual health because it leads to a debilitating sense of injustice that threatens our own progress in generosity.

Rather than feel injustice, the more appropriate response would be pity, which is how we would view the nondonor if we saw the situation from a spiritual perspective. The lack of giving is a mere symptom of a deeper issue. In my experience with parishes and their members, I see a correlation between spiritual maturity and financial support. If an individual's heart is enflamed by faith, it's extremely rare to find that they are a nondonor. They may be a modest donor relative to their income, especially in cases where they are still struggling to attain the virtue of generosity, but generally they give something.

The nondonor is another case. We spend our money on those things of value to us, and the nondonor is saying something about his relationship with the Church. Jesus alluded to this when he told the crowds, "For where your treasure is, there will your heart be also" (Mt 6:21).

About 30 to 40 percent of most congregations are non-donors, for a variety of reasons. Some people join a particular parish to get married in a beautiful setting or to baptize a child, but from day one rarely attend weekly liturgy. In other cases, the nondonor attends intermittently but hasn't yet fully embraced their faith. Still other nondonors used to be weekly attendees, but over time gradually grew lax in their observance. It's usually a long process. We used to speak of "fallen-away Catholics." It would be more accurate to speak of fellow parishioners who "slipped away." In many cases, they gradually found their way to the exits because of their lack of meaningful involvement in the parish.

In this light, it's okay to be distressed about the nongiver but don't be concerned about the money. First be concerned about the soul. If someone had reached out, and invited them to use their skills for the betterment of the community, the resulting relationships would in most cases have kept them in the parish and served as an opportunity to deepen their faith.

****

I didn't always see it this way. Having worked in many parishes, I used to grow angry and self-righteous at the thought that in every parish a large proportion of households essentially sailed for free. I naïvely determined to apply my marketing skills to turn the situation around.

My first step in that marketing plan was a focus group with nondonors to find out why they didn't give. There were many possible reasons, and I wanted to know what drove the decision. Did they not feel a true part of the congregation? Is that why they didn't give? Or was it simply a case where they didn't think about the expense of maintaining a large building? Maybe they didn't realize the parish needed their support. I was also willing to entertain the possibility that perhaps a certain segment of the population was so poor that they had nothing to give or that their ability to give looked so immaterial to the overall budget of the parish that they simply said, "Why bother?"

I was fortunate to have about a half-dozen households represented in a focus group one evening. The format was informal conversation over coffee and cookies, and the cardinal rule as moderator was "big ears, no judgment." My role was to listen and learn. I knew if I showed any displeasure whatsoever with any of the answers, people would immediately clam up, defeating the purpose of the group.

The second rule of moderating any focus group is to not telegraph a desired response. For example, if a focus group is brought together to determine whether people like a new toothpaste, the moderator wouldn't say, "We want to know whether you like our new brand X over the old brand Y." Making such a statement would prejudice the answer: out of politeness, some people won't say your new toothpaste tastes like shoe polish. They'll just smile and nod in agreement at its wonderful properties, and the marketer will later lose a bundle distributing a product that doesn't sell. Instead, the purpose of the group is couched in broader language, without the true intention revealed. In short, obtaining honest answers requires a bit of deception.

That's why my opening questions that evening were relatively vague. I inquired about things the participants liked and disliked about the parish, which led to a conversation about specific parish programs. That, in turn, moved very naturally to a discussion concerning paying for those programs. At this point, I glanced at the clock. We were now thirty minutes into what I promised would be a one-hour meeting, and I was just starting the topic of primary interest to me. "You've told me about those programs you like. If you were on the Finance Council, how would you pay for them?"

A single mother was quick to speak up. Sharp enough to see where the conversation was going, she chose the old "head 'em off at the pass" strategy. She explained the difficulty of raising a son alone, talked about the high cost of living, and concluded, "There are some of us who just can't afford to give anything. There is nothing left to give." Many nodded in sympathy, and I suggested it would be a good time for a short break to refill the coffee pot.

A few participants milled about to stretch their legs, and the usual small talk ensued among those still seated. Someone asked the mother whether she planned to take her son to the Disney road show coming to town.

"Oh, we saw it in Orlando last winter," she replied with her face aglow. As I returned with the coffee, the lady was gushing about what a fantastic time they had, with accommodations right on the park grounds, VIP passes, and a week in the sunshine. She was clearly bound up in the joy of remembering.

Waiting for the rest of the group to return, I took my seat at the table and joined in the conversation. "Did you happen to go to Universal Studios?" I asked. This only heightened her enthusiasm. "My son loved Universal Studios, but Sea World was the best!" With everyone seated and ready to resume, I waited as she went on to recount the last chapter of her vacation — the Pirates Dinner Adventure.

"Good for you," I finally intervened, hoping to get back on track before the subscribed hour had expired. "I'm sure your son will remember this trip for the rest of his life."

Of course, in her enthusiasm the woman didn't realize the awkward position she had placed both of us. She had just told the group she had nothing to give the church, then went on to describe a first-class trip that likely cost thousands in airfare, hotel, and theme-park tickets. I didn't want to embarrass her by pressing too many more questions, but on the other hand we were getting to the point of the conversation that would yield real insights.

Trying to avoid eye contact with the joyous vacationer, I returned the group to the conversation we had begun prior to the break. "Do people think they ought to at least give *something*?" I asked gingerly, fully expecting my new friend to remain silent on this issue. Instead, she was again the first to speak, referencing a sample appeal letter I had passed out earlier.

"It depends on how we're asked," she explained. "In this letter you say, 'Stewardship is trust in God's promises.' I think you need to realize you have different people with different levels of spirituality. This would be geared toward someone who exercises it every day, religiously. For those that don't, I think a more practical approach would be better."

"A more practical approach?" I queried.

"Yes," she replied with no little authority. "You almost have to look at your list of people and say, 'Okay, how active are these people in our church?' You might send one kind of letter to them, and for others that aren't as active — stay away from the whole spiritual end of it. This would be like pushing too much religion on them."

"So stay away from the spiritual aspects of giving?" I asked, just to be clear.

"I would," she said with a sincerity that couldn't be questioned. "People don't want too much religion with their religion."

The wording may have been less than elegant, but the point was clear: a certain portion of the population wants a religion that comforts without challenge. They "don't want too much religion with their religion."

****

As odd as this sounds, I have to admit at times I share this sentiment. I, too, am uncomfortable with the challenges of faith, especially when confronted with the Parable of the Workers and the Vineyard.

> "The kingdom of heaven is like a house-
> holder who went out early in the morn-
> ing to hire laborers for his vineyard. After
> agreeing with the laborers for a denarius a

day, he sent them into his vineyard. And going out about the third hour he saw others standing idle in the market place; and to them he said, 'You go into the vineyard too, and whatever is right I will give you.' So they went. Going out again about the sixth hour and the ninth hour, he did the same. And about the eleventh hour he went out and found others standing; and he said to them, 'Why do you stand here idle all day?' They said to him, 'Because no one has hired us.' He said to them, 'You go into the vineyard too.' And when evening came, the owner of the vineyard said to his steward, 'Call the laborers and pay them their wages, beginning with the last, up to the first.' And when those hired about the eleventh hour came, each of them received a denarius. Now when the first came, they thought they would receive more; but each of them also received a denarius. And on receiving it they grumbled at the householder, saying, 'These last worked only one hour, and you have made them equal to us who have borne the burden of the day and the scorching heat.' But he replied to one of them, 'Friend, I am doing you no wrong; did you not agree with me for a denarius? Take what belongs to you, and go; I choose to give to this last as I give to you. Am I not allowed to do what I choose with what belongs to me? Or do you begrudge my generosity?' So the last will be first, and the first last." (Mt 20:1–16)

This parable is hard to accept for those that give both time and money, and have been doing so for many years with full knowledge that others have not. There is a temptation to begrudge noncontributors and ask, "Why should I give more when others give nothing?"

When tempted with this thought, it's important to remember that the likely reason nondonors fall into this category is simple: most just haven't fully embraced God yet. They are still at a point where they "don't want too much religion with their religion." Like the workers hanging out until the eleventh hour, no one has approached them to hire them, to say, "You go into the vineyard, too."

Many will "enter the vineyard" — eventually. It just takes time to develop a spiritual understanding of generosity. Those who already give sacrificially must be patient without growing upset at the thought that others may one day come late to the party and still enjoy God's gracious mercy.

I have to admit this parable makes me uncomfortable. Whenever I read it, I come away feeling like the older brother in the Parable of the Prodigal Son, the one who got suckered into working while his younger brother went off to party away his share of the inheritance. But then I catch myself short, remembering it is God's love to give away as he sees fit. Any other attitude is to begrudge God's generosity.

Why should I give more when others give nothing? Because God has already given me everything.

FOR REFLECTION

This chapter explains three common temptations against generosity:

- "I don't make enough to give anything to charity."
- "I already give more than others."
- "Why should I give more when others give nothing?"

1. Have you ever caught yourself expressing these same sentiments? In a short paragraph, list the temptation against generosity that plagues you the most. Why is this so difficult for you? In light of the Scripture passages contained in this chapter, how would Jesus ask us to view our giving?

2. Share these thoughts with your money partner.

Chapter 9

⌐⌐

The Epic Battle:
Mercy versus Envy

All great summer movies, the blockbusters, boil down to one recurring theme: the struggle of good versus evil. Take your pick: Superhero versus Villain; The Force versus The Empire; The Righteous Individual versus Corrupt Society. Beneath every great storyline we ultimately find the same narrative retold with different characters. We just can't get enough of this stuff.

In striving for the virtue of generosity, this same struggle of good versus evil plays out in the deepest recesses of the heart. If we are to make peace with money, and overcome anxiety, this is where it will happen: in a battle not just between the opposing forces of generosity and greed, but between divine mercy and satanic envy. Like the characters in a summer blockbuster, we must ultimately choose between the two.

This sounds melodramatic, but I've chosen my words carefully. Changing external behavior is not enough. Beneath every action lies a deeper motivation, and it's this internal encounter that St. John of the Cross refers to as the second dark night, the "dark night of the soul." To make peace with money, we must change not only exterior actions — replacing greed with generosity — but also interior motivations — replacing envy with mercy. This is the more difficult task because it requires heroic humility to see ourselves at the level of motivation. For us to become truly free, this is where God must be allowed to do his work.

There exists between mercy and envy an eternal tug of war, reenacted every day in countless ways, if we have eyes to see such things. Too often we don't. Love is a whisper, and the daily encounter of mercy goes unnoticed — until we look for it.

****

My wife's grandfather passed away in 2009 at the age of one hundred one. Grandpa Aberle was married in the midst of the Great Depression, and lived through the dustbowl days of the 1930s when the high plains were reduced to nothing but thistles and grasshoppers. He was short and stocky, and active in gardening well into his nineties. He loved his house and little plot of land in Napoleon, North Dakota, and would proudly share the garden's produce. His eyesight never failed, and somewhere around his ninety-sixth birthday he proved it by waxing my father-in-law and me in a game of billiards.

But nature eventually leaves no one untouched, and about the time Grandpa's independence began to fail, so too did the agricultural economy. By the turn of the millennium it became increasingly clear that the true "family farm" would soon be a thing of the past.

That's a tough thing to watch. In July 2002, Stella and I had gone out to her parents' farm to help with field work. By this point, four of Markus and Helen's five children had already left the farm and the last was readying to head to college. That was why temporary labor from the cities — including Stella and me — had become an annual necessity. I didn't mind spending a week out on the prairie; sometimes it feels good to get dirty and tired. But on this particular evening I had had my fill. It was one of those upper-ninety-degree days with an incessant forty-knot west wind, the kind that strips every bit of moisture from the land and leaves the eyes of man and beast red and squinting.

In July, the sun sets well after nine o'clock, so it was late before I finished my field work and returned to the farmstead. Helen, my mother-in-law, had come in from milking cows, and I could tell she was in great pain. Seven days a week, for forty years, she put on her black rubber boots and made the trek to the barn to do chores, first at five in the morning and a second time around four in the afternoon. It's hard work. If you're the romantic type, forget the images of family dairies you may have seen in ice cream commercials. Cows are dumb, filthy, dangerous beasts, and reaching beneath sixty animals twice every day is a brutal regimen that had taken its toll on Helen's back. The doctor told her if she continued to do the milking she would one day be crippled.

"Has Markus come in for dinner?" I gingerly asked her. "No," she answered and said nothing more. I could tell from her voice and her limp that she was, in the brisk vernacular of farm life, "shot." So I quietly made sandwiches, reluctantly resolved to finally have "the talk" with Markus, a conversation I had been planning for some time. It wasn't a matter of *whether* he was going to get out of farming: it was a matter of *when*. After seeing how the drought that summer had devastated the land, I was certain that each passing year would only be a further set-back. The pain on Helen's face was final proof that the time for change had arrived. "When" became "now."

Straddling the four-wheeler, I pulled out of the farmstead onto the gravel road with a lunch bucket wedged between my legs. Hordes of grasshoppers scattered before me, reminding me of Grandpa Aberle's stories of the 1930s when a shirt tossed aside in the heat of the day would be gone by evening, eaten by swarms of the pests. But even this frightful thought couldn't ruin the moment. The sun had set, giving way to the ever-so-slow twilight that's a hallmark of the high plains. As the summer sun receded, so too did the wind and the heat, a pattern common in the Dakotas. It's as though God says, "Okay, enough already" and relents, another of his silent mercies.

I found Markus about two miles south of the farm. Because of the drought, he and other farmers had gotten a waiver to cut and bale whatever vegetation had managed to grow on their Conservation Reserve Program land. It was an emergency measure, one needed to feed their cattle. Markus was about a quarter mile out, and as his tractor grew near, I could see the thistles and tall prairie grass give way beneath the blade.

As he got closer, I lifted up the lunch pail, signaling break time. The man lived on Pepsi and cigarettes, and I knew the sandwich might be the first nutritious thing he'd had all day. A broad smile revealed black creases around his eyes where summer sweat and the day's wind had done their art work. I should have brought a wet rag.

"How's it going?" I asked as he shut off the tractor. "Can't complain," he answered, reaching for what likely was his sixth Pepsi of the day. This was classic Markus. He never did actually complain, and that would be part of the challenge I faced.

After we had finished the sandwiches, I offered my opinion that maybe this should be the last season, that maybe it was time to get out of farming. I went through the whole list of reasons, starting with the drought and commodity prices, and ending by reminding him how tough dairy farming had become for Helen.

"I think if she thought about it, she would realize just how good she has it," countered Markus. His comment left me silent. I had rehearsed this conversation for quite some time, but this was an answer I hadn't foreseen.

I should have known better. Markus had farmed since he was fourteen and — I'm sure — at the age of fifty-five the prospect of starting a whole new life was not something he wanted to think about. On top of it all, the evening had grown perfectly peaceful, with a pink sky that did nothing but encourage the meadowlarks. In every direction to the horizon, the only sound was that made by nature. I looked around. Whatever sadness I felt at the thought of giving up the farm had to have been only a fraction of what he was feeling. There was a long man-silence between us.

If I had to pick a moment that marked "the beginning of the end" for Markus and Helen's life on the farm, this would be it. From this point forward, the levers were set in motion to eventually leave farming. That winter Markus would start a factory job in Fargo, three hours to the east, and leave farming for good. But there were complications. Helen's parents were both in their nineties, and it seemed wrong to her to leave them behind in Napoleon, especially when her parents likely had little time left on this earth. She decided she would stay behind to care for them — with her fifth child soon off to college and now her husband gone, too.

At that point, no one could have guessed it would be six years before her mother passed away, and seven for her father. With each year, more of Helen's neighbors left their farms, as the depopulation of the prairie continued unabated. Even the country church where the family had worshiped for decades was closed and ceremoniously burned to the ground, giving the ashes back to the earth. As the years passed, I began to wonder whether she felt the same isolation as those who first settled the land.

Imagine the heart filled with mercy that would take on such a burden, to fulfill the fourth commandment to "honor your father and your mother" (Ex 20:12). This is what I mean when I say love is a whisper. I have to believe this sort of sacrificial love is as common as the air we breathe, but no more noticed or appreciated.

****

To love this deeply comes at a price. And it is in paying this price that mercy and envy do battle. To understand their interplay, let's first be clear on terms.

In the words of the *Catechism of the Catholic Church*: "Envy is a capital sin. It refers to the sadness at the sight of another's goods and the immoderate desire to acquire them for oneself, even unjustly. When it wishes grave harm to a neighbor it is a mortal sin" (CCC 2539).

Envy is much worse than jealousy. Jealousy sees what another has, and desires it for oneself. Envy sees what another has, *and wishes they didn't have it.* That's a big difference. Jealousy pales beside envy.

As for mercy, we sometimes think of it as a synonym for forgiveness. But in broader terms, mercy is more than that; it is nothing short of heroic love. To participate in God's Divine Mercy is to pour out every ounce of strength, to love beyond our human capacity. Without Christ, this is not possible. But having first experienced God's mercy ourselves, having tasted supernatural love, man is able to "love beyond love." This is the fertile soil that gave life to Helen's selfless care for her parents.

Such love does not go unnoticed by the Tempter. The moment we take our eyes off God, fatigue prompts us to look at others who don't carry the burden we do and to ask, "Why me? Why have I chosen to love this deeply? Does anyone notice? Does anyone care?" With these thoughts in mind, we stand at the precipice of allowing our acts of mercy to be swallowed up by envy. Too tired to expend additional energy to encourage others to join the effort; *there is a bitter temptation to wish others' good circumstances diminished.* You can almost hear Satan's prodding: "Why should another's life be so much more pleasant than your own?" It takes extraordinary grace to avoid resentment and self-pity. Without God, the person inclined toward compassion is tempted to exchange mercy for envy.

As we give of ourselves, we feel the cost of that love, and the more tempting it becomes to quit. It's like a children's game you might see at a summer county fair.

Tethered to bungee ropes, children run toward a goal to win a prize, but the further they stretch the ropes, the more resistance they feel until — only inches from their goal — they fall on their bottoms and are sprung backward. This is what makes the battle of mercy versus envy high drama. Christ's mercy urges us forward; envy pulls us back.

Earlier I referred earlier to envy as "satanic." I have good company in that assessment. After defining envy, the *Catechism of the Catholic Church* notes: "St. Augustine saw envy as '*the* diabolical sin.' [And St. Gregory the Great wrote:] 'From envy are born hatred, detraction, calumny, joy caused by the misfortune of a neighbor, and displeasure caused by his prosperity'" (CCC 2539).

We see this envious displeasure at another's good fortune in the Parable of the Prodigal Son (Lk 15:11–32). Typically, this story is held up as a quintessential example of mercy, and rightly so. But it is equally helpful at illustrating mercy's lethal enemy: envy.

The younger of two sons asks his father for his share of the inheritance, which he squanders on dissolute living in a foreign land. Faced with hunger and shame, he eventually returns home, prepared to apologize. While still at a distance, his father spots him, and without waiting for his son to ask forgiveness, runs toward him. Before the son can complete an apology, the father is calling servants to prepare a party, "For this son was dead, and is alive again, he was lost, and is found" (Lk 15:24).

After the father's act of mercy, the focus shifts to the envy of the older brother who has grown indignant at his father's response. Even after his father tells him, "All that is mine is yours" (Lk 15:31), the older son is still not satisfied. If he were merely jealous — wanting what his younger brother had — the father's offer would have sufficed. But he was more than jealous; he was envious. It wasn't enough to gain what his younger brother had, and more. He wanted to see good things taken away from a brother he judged undeserving. In the final analysis, the parable pits the father's mercy against the older son's envy. It is this juxtaposition of mercy versus envy that gives the parable its enduring plot.

But there's more. What makes the story tragic, in a Shakespearean sort of way, is a deficiency in the older brother. His response suggests that he never felt his father's love, a love that had been there all along. This renders the son's service nothing more than the keeping of a social contract by a dutiful child. Because he does not see the love that his father has for him, he is not able to extend mercy to his younger brother and so he succumbs to envy.

Still, we are naturally sympathetic to the older brother's feelings. Whenever I hear this parable, I instinctively find a part of me siding with the older brother, who appears at first glance to be defensible in his anger. He's not. To think otherwise is to fall into Satan's trap. Envy is diabolical because it exhibits the characteristics of Satan, the Father of Lies, whose favorite trick is cloaking evil in a seeming good. In this case, evil intent — wishing ill upon his brother — is coated in a veneer of apparent justice: why should the younger brother have enjoyed what he did not earn? Recall the earlier analogy of sin as sour candy encrusted in sugar. The heart's ill intent is the sour candy; righteous indignation is the sugar coating. Beware:

the Father of Lies can dress up even a mortal sin like envy, twisting it to make it appear as a virtue.

There is a second caution woven within this parable. Note how one person's sin can lead another to stumble as well. The fall of both brothers began with the sin of the younger one, who squandered the family's hard-earned wealth on loose living. His sin of excess and fornication scandalized his older brother, who probably spent many a night fuming about his sibling's sinful ways. Unaware of his father's love for him, in due time indignation grew into envy. Now, rather than one brother in sin, there were two.

This same dynamic can be seen in today's society. In a world where there is great discrepancy in the distribution of wealth, envy is understandably common, but no less ugly than greed. As the saying goes, two wrongs don't make a right. Greed in one person never justifies envy in another. Yet, too often we allow conspicuous consumption by others to tempt us to envy, to wish ill upon those who have more than us.

This sin gets woven into our actions in very subtle ways. For example, imagine mercy-hearted people who see wealth consolidated among the top 5 percent of citizens, while neighbors go without food or medical care. It would be natural for people of good will to feel a certain indignation about an unjust economic system.

In response, many advocate for a redistribution of wealth through the tax code. Fair enough, but this is the point at which honesty with oneself is crucial. Is this advocacy driven purely by mercy for the poor, or does it contain traces of envy of the rich? To determine the real motivation, we must begin with an examination of our own actions. To come out on the side of the angels, the hallmark of mercy is this: the advocate for taxes has first voluntarily tithed on his own income.[15] If not, chances are that the advocacy is driven not by mercy, but also to some degree by envy. These advocates not only want to help the poor, but find a certain pleasure in bringing the wealthy down a notch or two.

Advocacy that "someone *else* do something" is common, even celebrated, which will forever strike me as odd. For example, there is a temptation to say, "I would be willing to help others and pay higher taxes if everyone else does, too." Why wait for others? Why not do what you can *now*? Imagine if Christ merely advocated that someone else go to the cross. Likewise, imagine if Jesus had said, "I'll go to the cross, but I'm not going unless everyone comes with me!" Love doesn't wait for others to do the good and just thing, and only then join in. Love leads. My point: the pure of heart will always give first from their own account, and give generously, before suggesting that others give more. If animated by true divine mercy, our actions will be in the category of both/and. We would begin by giving alms, immediately, to save even a few, then go on to advocate for larger issues of social justice.

We find a great irony when it comes to the battle between mercy and envy. In response to a world that is hurting, God ever more generously pours out the gift of mercy. But here's the rub: the demands of love test the compassionate person. Unless firmly rooted in Christ, the "mercy-person" can easily succumb to envy. Those who fall generally do so because they recognize the gift of mercy in their own heart, but reject the God who placed it there.

This is the saddest of circumstances: good seed on rootless, rocky soil.

The initial motivation to compassion is just the starting point. To avoid the temptation of envy, we need God's ongoing grace. Again I refer to what Monsignor Merth taught his second graders: "God loves me." We respond to the love that found us first. This is the love that softens hearts, not only toward the poor, but toward the rich, also. God wants to bring both to salvation. Too often we would be happy to save one and damn the other, not realizing that the material poverty of one person is linked to the spiritual poverty of another.

This brings us full circle to the discussion of the necessity of ongoing conversion. Without God's constant grace softening the heart, the initial gift of mercy begins to atrophy, and we find ourselves bitter with envy like the parable's older brother, rather than filled with divine mercy like his father.

Thankfully, there is an antidote, and it works equally well whether we suffer from greed or envy. In the next chapter we explore the all-purpose balm that softens hearts.

FOR REFLECTION

In this chapter we said, "In a world where there is great discrepancy in the distribution of wealth, envy is understandably common, but no less ugly than greed. As the saying goes, two wrongs don't make a right. Greed in one person never justifies envy in another. Yet, too often we allow conspicuous consumption by others to tempt us to envy, to wish ill upon those who have more than us."

The following exercise is difficult, but necessary. Answer these questions with intense honesty:

1. Have you ever felt envy? Beyond wishing that you possessed something, have you ever wished that someone else *did not* have something? In a short paragraph, describe the circumstances.

2. Envy is *the single biggest factor* that stops people from making peace with money. Share what you wrote with your money partner, and ask him or her to suggest ways — in light of the discussion in this chapter — you can overcome feelings of envy.

Chapter 10

Greed and Gratitude

Everything you own you will one day give away. The only question is to whom you will give it, and whether it will be with a warm hand or a cold one.

In this light, it is puzzling to me why amassing great wealth, for its own sake, would be anyone's lifetime goal. You would think people clever enough to stash away a million dollars would be smart enough to realize they can't take it with them to the grave.

Even so, the pursuit of wealth continues. Worse still, there is a growing discrepancy between the ultra-wealthy and those whose work helps them achieve financial notoriety. The Economic Policy Institute reports, "In 1965, U.S. CEOs in major companies earned 24 times more than a typical worker; this ratio grew to 35 in 1978 and to 71 in 1989.... By 2007 [CEO pay] was 275 times that of the typical worker. In other words, in 2007 a CEO earned more in one workday (there are 260 in a year) than the typical worker earned all year."[16]

Today it's not difficult to find examples of top corporate executives making total annual compensation of $30 million or more. This gives us much to ponder. To begin, why would anyone want to make that kind of money, especially in light of our earlier discussion about the illusory nature of wealth? Whether $5 million, $15 million, or $30 million, does it really change one's lifestyle in any meaningful way? Does the person making $30 million a year eat better than the guy making a mere $5 million? Does he dress better? Drive a nicer car? Have a bigger TV or more cell-phone minutes? To recall an earlier discussion, at $5 million a year it's safe to say one's material needs and wants will probably be satisfied. There is no reason to want more. Desiring a $30 million annual salary is simply illogical; there is little more that can be said.

So let's move on to another, more interesting, question: How can anyone justify it? How is it possible for an individual to believe he or she is actually worth a salary of that magnitude? Why is the pay gap not a grave embarrassment to him or her? What kind of ego must it take to believe a multimillion dollar salary is justified by anyone? And is there a remedy? To answer these questions, we'll examine erroneous assumptions that have become prevalent in our society.

****

In 1989 I was fortunate to be able to sing with the Notre Dame Folk Choir. As part of a recording project, we traveled to Gethsemani Abbey, a Trappist monastery in Kentucky. It was one of those great trips that college students often enjoy, but rarely appreciate until decades later. All we had to do for a week was sing, hang out, and pray — nice work if you can get it. There were also reflection talks each day, and an occasional sidebar conversation with a monk.

I recall one of those chance encounters with a brother whose name has long since escaped me. It was a short conversation, little more than a greeting, but when he learned that I was in business school, he offered an unsolicited observation. "The main spiritual problem we have in America today," he mused, "is that as a society we have confused what we do with who we are." Reading the puzzled look on my face, he paused, and for good measure, repeated himself as he returned to his work in the garden.

Some twenty years later, with more life experience, I now understand and agree with his observation. To the brother's point, work provides more than a paycheck. It gives us social standing, respect, and deference from others — or the opposite, depending upon the job. Because of these social reinforcements, both positive and negative, society links *what we do* with *who we are*. This is the first erroneous assumption that plagues our thinking.

Upon reflection, it's odd that society affords more respect to those with certain careers or job titles. It is very possible to be either a successful, wealthy scoundrel, or a poor, forever-failing one. Scoundrels come in both flavors. It's also possible to be a successful, wealthy saint, or a poor, uneducated one. Saints, too, can be found among both the rich and the poor; character is independent of what one does for a living or how much one makes. Thus, the good brother cautioned that we not confuse *what we do (our job)* with *who we are (our character)*.

To live in this confusion has sad consequences, particularly for the person seeking fulfillment solely in career advancement. The real or imagined prestige we get from careers and positions — from what we do — ultimately never satisfies because it comes from the outside to puff us up like cotton candy.

****

When I was a still a little child, my father took me to the circus and bought a big, pink, fluffy hair-ball of sweetness for me. As he put the cardboard holder in my hands, I wondered how it was possible for so small a kid to eat such a large bale of candy — until I bit into it and discovered there was virtually nothing there. It just melted away. The person who relies on career, position, and honors for self-esteem is like cotton candy; from a distance, impressive in size, even daunting, with an imagined importance that pleases the eye; but in interpersonal relationship he melts away for lack of substance.

I make this analogy with nothing but compassion for such a soul. For decades, the mantra of self-esteem has infused educators and parents with the notion that if we just told young people often enough how wonderful they were, if we gave them enough exterior reinforcement in the form of praise and honors, this alone would suffice to steel them against poor life decisions. It doesn't. Character is built from the inside out, not from the outside in.

Sister Marietta taught us this in high school. She began class by announcing that no amount of praise, basketball championships, lovely girlfriends, academic honors, or money could ever give us self-esteem. She then crossed her arms and inserted a long, dramatic pause, leaving the class hanging. I looked around at my classmates, who were equally stumped. What else was there in our teenage world?

Great teaching always includes a bit of theater, and Sister Marietta knew just the right moment to finally answer her own question. "The way you build self-esteem is to make decisions every day that you can be proud of." This, of course, meant moral decisions, doing the right thing, and she would spend the rest of the semester telling us what that might be.

Sister also explained that money, honors, and status depend to varying degrees on others and so they can be lost. But character, painstakingly built day by day in the pursuit of holiness, is within our control. Unlike jobs, promotions, and investments, a righteous character can't be taken away, only forfeited through immoral actions. In essence, Sister Marietta and the Trappist brother at Gethsemani were saying the same thing: don't confuse career, honors, and possessions with character. Don't confuse *what we do* with *who we are*.

****

Now let's return to our earlier question: "How is it possible for an individual to believe he or she is actually worth a multimillion dollar salary? How does that person justify it?"

The justification comes in two steps. First, people confuse *what they do* with *who they are*. This first mistake leads to a second. We confuse our *talents and abilities* with the *situation* in which we work. In the final analysis, it is this false corollary that allows individuals to justify huge salaries, and sidestep an examination of conscience that confronts their own greed.

We'll use a fictional Mrs. Jones as an example. She heads a very large corporation with annual sales of $50 billion and profits of $3 billion. Given the magnitude of the business, she feels justified in collecting an annual paycheck of $30 million. Individuals, and the boards that set their compensation, rationalize such salaries based upon what the individual purportedly earns for the company and shareholders. Relative to a profit of $3 billion, $30 million is a modest number. Thus, Mrs. Jones feels justified in negotiating such extraordinary compensation. But there is a fly in the ointment. This rationale confuses Mrs. Jones' inherent talent — which, granted, may be considerable — with the situation in which she works.

To illustrate further, let's bring the numbers down to a more human level. As a fund-raising consultant, if I lead a parish campaign with a relatively modest $500,000 goal, the most I can reasonably charge is about $35,000. But if I consult on a private school campaign in a much wealthier neighborhood that has the potential for a $5 million goal, I could likely propose $350,000 in fees and still secure the board's approval — for essentially the same amount of time and effort as the other engagement. Because I'm now making ten times more money, am I ten times smarter? Ten times more experienced? No. I'm the same person, with the same skills, simply working in a different situation, so why would the school pay me ten times more for the same work? It's because society has bought into the false assumption that we are what we do, and if what we do makes ten times more money than the next guy, then we must be ten times smarter. And if ten times smarter, then worth a salary ten times as much. *We confuse our innate talents and abilities with the situation in which we work.* This, I believe, is the flawed circular reasoning that allows individuals to intrinsically justify salaries that defy comprehension. Conveniently, it helps us sidestep any questions our conscience might raise about greed.

****

There is concern these days that the greater society is getting "ripped off" by those who continue to justify unimaginable salaries, an issue society attempts to solve through political means. My concern is, first and foremost, the soul of the individual who fails to see or acknowledge greed. This is the proper starting point and, in the final analysis, the only approach that has any real hope of succeeding. Which is easier: thousands of pages of legal regulations, which will forever have loopholes or the conversion of one soul? The person who has undergone true conversion, who has overcome greed, does not need civil law to rein in his or her behavior. If our fictional Mrs. Jones was truly striving for holiness, she herself would be working to uproot greed from her soul and a solution imposed from the outside would not be needed.

The problem, of course, is this: while Mrs. Jones may be fictional, thousands of others are not. They have confused *what they do* with *who they are*, and have no self-awareness of the greed deep in their bones.

From this perspective, it seems odd that the Church often speaks of a "preferential option for the poor." Is the soul of the CEO any less important than the janitor who cleans her office each night?

What's more, imagine the extraordinary good that one CEO has within her power, if her soul were passionately converted to Christ. That done, we might begin to make a real dent in the stated "preferential option for the poor." The two are inextricably linked. We seem to overlook the fact that the spiritual poverty of one member of the Body of Christ has a direct impact on the material poverty of many others. We have lost sight of the need for conversion on a personal level. Instead, many Church leaders, academics, and politicians continue to speak of a vague social justice that often does little more than provide cover for not confronting our own need for conversion.

As long as we talk about "social justice," we are talking about someone else, about societal "structures" and "immoral systems." That's within our comfort zone. But to talk about my own need for conversion, about my personal inclination toward greed? To acknowledge the part I play? That takes real personal courage, and few of us are ready to engage on this level.

Imagine if we replaced the language of "social justice" with that of "personal justice." What if, instead of speaking of "unjust social structures," we examined "unjust personal behaviors"? Again, this is the proper starting point. Society is made up of individuals. To have any hope of changing social structures, we need individuals willing to embrace their own call to holiness.

****

To aid this effort, I suggest a twofold spiritual remedy: A new understanding of work and a renewed effort to lead a life marked by generosity and gratitude. Most of us have a limited view of work, which sees our labor in terms of a paycheck and personal fulfillment. A Christian perspective sees a larger aim, best summarized in the Jesuit motto *"Ad Majorem Dei Gloriam"* (For the Greater Glory of God).

In this worldview, the Christian's true boss is God. We work for more than a paycheck; we're privileged to be God's hands and feet. Recall the conversation about farmers in chapter 2. Most family farmers I know see their labor as a corporal work of mercy: feeding the hungry. Given the long hours, risk, and minimal financial reward, this view is the only one that makes sense.

Understood and properly executed, all work — from the most menial task to the most sophisticated — can be experienced as a participation in building up the kingdom of God. This idea is easy to grasp for those whose jobs are directly related to the corporal works of mercy, who daily meet the physical and emotional needs of fellow citizens. But others, too, do their part. Case in point: my friend sells athletic gear for a living, and he sees his work as God's work. Consider the health benefits of exercise and the community-building excitement of Friday night competition. In my buddy's world, sweat socks and helmets are part of God's bountiful plan for a healthy, happy life as the Creator intended. That's part of the satisfaction he finds in his daily routine.

With a modicum of reflection, most of us could find the same spiritual satisfaction in our work. Not only would our labor be more fulfilling and less stressful, the underlying attitude of serving God would help keep greed in check.

Unfortunately, few want to venture down this path, and I can't say I blame them. Jesus didn't ingratiate himself when he likened his followers to lowly servants. "Let your loins be girded and your lamps burning, and be like men who are waiting for their master to come home from the marriage feast, so that they may open to him at once when he comes and knocks" (Lk 12:35–36). This is one of those scripture passages many of us would prefer to skip over. Waiting on a master is not the professional image we would like to have of ourselves.

St. Paul takes the challenge one step further when he tells the Corinthians they are slaves of Christ (see 1 Cor 7:22). That's drastic language. I'm not just a servant, but a slave. To think of myself in this way requires a radical new mind-set. As Christ's slave, I have no right to expect anything — everything I have is a gratuitous gift from God. No wonder people are averse to seeing their work as first and foremost for Christ. Who wants to be a slave? To see ourselves as servant and slave is to understand there is no entitlement that comes from pleasing him, no quid pro quo, no tit for tat. This is very difficult to understand, because as a society we are so focused on the material exchange of time and talent for money and benefits. Of course, we still need money to care for our families. It's true that "every worker deserves his wage" (1 Tim 5:18) and "now to one who works, his wages are not reckoned as a gift but as his due" (Rom 4:4).

At the same time, when our labor is elevated to the realm of serving one we love, the paradigm in which we work is enlarged beyond "I did this, so I deserve that!" Instead, our work becomes a gift to God, and our material possessions a return gift from him. Work is elevated from meager contract to the realm of love's joyful duty. Isn't that better than what we have now?

****

Marriage provides a good example of service from a Christian worldview. Would I negotiate with my wife before I cooked dinner for her? Would I demand that the favor be repaid? Would I want a guarantee in writing? Of course not. I cook dinner out of love, as a gift to her, and on Saturday she will likely return the favor by doing laundry in the same spirit. But to expect Stella to do laundry, to think that my cooking dinner gave me the right to demand compensation in the form of a return favor, takes what would have been an act of love — cooking dinner — and turns it into a quid pro quo based on my own needs and wants, on calculated greed.

The question, then, boils down to this: Do we want our work to remain on the level of a mere transaction, where greed — always present in the human condition — tempts us to believe we deserve our possessions (even exorbitant salaries) on our own accord? Or do we choose to elevate our work, seeing it as an act of love for God and his children? If the latter, work will be done neither with a sense of entitlement nor a belief that I single-handedly merit the riches to which I lay claim. Rather, work becomes our gift to God in thanksgiving for his gifts to us. Our attitude is that of one who believes it is God who, out of love, ultimately supplies our needs.

It could be argued that this viewpoint is a recipe for creating a chump, someone society will be only too glad to take advantage of. To that charge I would ask a question: What is the measure of happiness and fulfillment? In business, I've had a few people take advantage of me. So what? Their greed is on their head. They will have to answer for it one day. If circumstances force you into doing business with people who revel in greed, there are two options. You can meet them on their playing field, adopt a similar stance, fight for every nickel, and fret about your share relative to theirs. Or you can say "X" is enough for my needs and just because I do business with greedy people I don't have to act like them. Preserve your character; safeguard your interior peace. And when tempted toward envy, say a prayer of thanksgiving for God's blessings.

Gratitude is always rooted in an underlying disposition of humility. Simply put, humble people are naturally grateful, and gratitude is the antidote to greed. This explains why the pay gap in this country continues to grow. It widens to the extent that humility — the prerequisite posture of the spiritual life — has declined in lockstep with the erosion of "organized" religion. This is the arid milieu that breeds individuals able to justify exorbitant salaries. Ironically, the very people who decry religion in the public sphere are often the same ones to rail against the inevitable result: greed unrestrained by humility. Unfortunately, their proposed remedy — regulation — will never fully tame the problem. Attempting to do so is trying to solve a spiritual issue through legal means.

At its root, the person who justifies an exorbitant salary has a spiritual challenge: he or she must strive for humility. Such a person has lost sight of the most basic truth any dusty farmer knows in his bones: we can't bring anything into being that doesn't already exist. We can't create matter from nothing. Humans can combine, fabricate, extrude, shape, design, and manufacture, but can't create something from nothing. This also applies beyond the realm of the physical: close your eyes and try to imagine a color you've never seen before. You'll find yourself describing your "new" color based upon something you've seen before. Man cannot bring into existence that which does not exist.

To go deeper, consider this fact from a first-person perspective. I exist. I could just as easily not exist. And if I did not exist there is nothing I could do on my own to bring myself into existence.

It follows, then, that I owe my existence to someone or something. My very life is a gift, and this gift of existence is infinitely more important than what I do. If I didn't exist I would be doing nothing! That's a painfully humbling thought. Yet we justify greed, and the excessive accumulation of wealth, based upon what we believe we have done to deserve it. *But without this initial gift of existence, I would have nothing else. Greed is ultimately a sin of pride that forgets this fundamental fact.*

Even in his day, St. Paul had to remind the Corinthians, "What have you that you did not receive? If then you received it, why do you boast as if it were not a gift?" (1 Cor 4:7). Everything we have begins with the initial gift of life. Without this gift, nothing else matters.

I don't expect this philosophy to radically permeate the heart in a lightning flash, though that could happen. Rather, it's my hope that even the soul desensitized by greed instinctively recognizes the importance of gratitude because from here we have a foothold for God to work.

Sadly, the odds are against us. When it comes to gratitude, our culture has grown sloppy in its use of the word "thank you." In many instances, it has become little more than a substitute for "good-bye" or a cue that a public announcement is finished. Rare, indeed, is the heartfelt "thank you" that acknowledges everything as a gift from God.

What we need is a radical witness to gratitude.

****

Tamee lives with her husband and six children — two boys and four girls — on the edge of an Indian reservation in the Minnesota north woods. I have never met a more grateful heart.

Her oldest is twelve, and the youngest, a set of twins, just turned two. Her husband has a modest but stable job in a nearby small town, and they make ends meet by raising chickens for meat and eggs, and tending to a large garden during the all-too-brief summer. They split wood to heat their rural four-square house, keep a goat in the pasture for milk, and tend bees for honey and extra cash. In the midst of all this, Tamee home schools the children.

If you have already begun to wonder how it all gets done, you would have an accurate picture of the daily drama. Of course, each child has a variety of assigned chores, from picking eggs to emptying the dishwasher, and if each performs that set of duties, all goes relatively well.

But life sometimes throws a curveball that no amount of organization can overcome.

Winter threatened to come early last fall, and Tamee was under pressure to get the summer's produce canned before a killing frost made three months of garden labor a moot point. Unfortunately, the electricity had gone out for several days that week, rendering her electric stove — a necessity for canning vegetables — useless. Of course, other electric appliances were also down. Tamee watched helplessly as the laundry piled up: diapers, socks, and a mountain of T-shirts and towels. To complicate matters, her oldest son had had a severe stomach ache for several days, limiting his ability to help around the house.

Then things took a turn for the worse. Six-year-old Zeanna developed a mysterious rash on her cheeks and nose. This was a medical condition Tamee had never seen before, right down to the fish-like smell emanating from the blisters. Other mothers began to call, complaining that their children were suffering from a similar rash. Alarmingly, it wasn't limited to one or two children in the area. Apparently, nearly everyone in Zeanna's home-school enrichment class had contracted the puzzling disease. What could it possibly be?

Periodically, home school families gather in the town of Park Rapids, about an hour away, so that the younger children can get together for supplemental classes such as art. The lesson that week was "color and texture." Parents were supposed to bring in fall leaves for the children to use in their art work, but — no surprise here — Tamee missed the email. Upon arriving at class and noticing the oversight, she did what any mother would do. She settled her children securely in class, and then went into the woods near the school to find the most beautiful leaves in the forest. Unknown to Tamee, in October that would be poison ivy.

Tamee gleefully returned with the most vibrant, fiery red leaves she had ever seen, and distributed them to the children along with the oaks, aspens, and other bounty of the forest brought in that day by other moms.

Of course, to experience texture, the art specialist encouraged the children to rub the leaves across their cheeks, and tickle their noses with the fine hairs on the back of the leaf. It was all so delightful.

The error, of course, was not discovered until the phone began to ring the next day. It wasn't long before Tamee realized that she was likely the source of the suffering. As the week wore on, she discovered that children in four other families had poison ivy troubles.

By the following Monday, things were not much better. The weather had turned decidedly colder, the children were playing on the forbidden hay bales, and a friend called to commiserate and remind Tamee that they both deserved something better. On top of it all, Tamee had awoken that morning to find a mouse nest in her chest-of-drawers, happily nestled with her undergarments. It was all too much. She reached for her coat, thinking, "I can't take it anymore. I've got to get out of this house!"

But as she reached for the door, a painful thought suddenly occurred to her. "Where would I go? Even if I had somewhere to go, it would take ninety minutes to get the children ready — that's just more work!"

Feeling helpless, she slumped down in the entryway and began to cry. "Then I felt God wrap his arms around me," recalled Tamee. "And I began to think, 'What does it matter? I have piles of dirty clothes because I have six beautiful children. I have a sink full of dishes because I have a garden full of food. And I have mice that want to live in my home because I have firewood and heat.'"

With these thoughts, her tears turned to laughter.

This is the redemptive power of radical gratitude.

FOR REFLECTION

Imagine seeing mice in your socks drawer, and using it as an occasion to thank God for a warm house. That's what I would call "radical gratitude."

1. List ten things for which you are thankful. Are any as radical as the example above? If not, list an eleventh item, and say a prayer of thanksgiving.

2. Share these thoughts with your money partner.

Chapter 11

Why Enough Is Never Enough

There is a common assumption these days that upon death all but the most troublesome individuals go directly to the arms of God. Since death still waits for me, I can't say from personal experience whether this is true or not. It is a lovely thought, however, and I'm sure it gives the surviving family no little comfort. But with just a little reflection, the assumption proves itself quite feeble. So much so, in fact, that it's curious how it gained such popularity.

Picture planning a dinner party for eight. To get the chemistry right, you are careful to invite guests who will enjoy each other's company. Indeed, if all arrive in a festive mood, and if everyone in the group is at peace with each other, the evening will be a memorable one. Now with this idyllic scene in mind, imagine two of the guests showing up at the dinner table after battling each other in court all week, each unaware the other would be there. Suddenly, the chemistry of the room changes. The entire group feels the tension. Gone is the festive party mood.

Now apply this imagery to heaven. Everyone is at peace with each other, happy and joyful in loving communion. But with our new policy of letting anyone in, ready or not, Joe comes through the golden gates prepared to pick an argument at the drop of a hat. Right behind him is Martha, an otherwise fine woman, but well known for her years as the town's most reliable gossip. Getting off the same bus is Tony, who never repented for a string of broken hearts caused by his well-practiced deception. And on it goes, busload after busload of welcome-to-heaven freebies. It wouldn't be long before heaven looked a lot like earth. As they say, "There goes the neighborhood."

Little wonder Jesus said, "You, therefore, must be perfect, as your heavenly Father is perfect" (Mt 5:48). This sounds like impossible idealism, but if my logic holds up, perfection is little more than the minimum requirement for admittance to the heavenly banquet. Heaven wouldn't be heaven if we had to spend eternity rubbing shoulders with unrepentant braggarts, gossips, thieves, liars, perverts, and scoundrels. That sounds more like earth than heaven. No, I'm pretty sure Jesus meant what he said.

In this light, the Catholic doctrine of purgatory is a welcome part of God's merciful plan. Purgatory gives those who strove for goodness in this life a final opportunity for purification so that we might enter heaven, even if we die before attaining the necessary perfection. This gives me hope. I don't want to be left outside heaven's proverbial gates. At the same time, I don't want to be welcomed in my current state, for fear I'd be the ornery duck ruining the celestial party. I want in, but I know I'm not ready yet.

So I struggle for holiness, even though I doubt I will have conquered my sins before I die.

And despite failure, I keep trying because I suspect it's less painful to be purified while on earth rather than in purgatory: "For now we see in a mirror dimly, but then face to face" (1 Cor 13:12). At present, we are spared seeing our souls directly; we see dimly, as in a first-century mirror. I think that's one of God's many acts of mercy. Though we recognize our sins, he allows us to strive for holiness without seeing or feeling their full impact. Thankfully, we still "see dimly." It's as though God allows us to recognize our faults while giving us a bit of anesthetic to lessen the pain. But that anesthetic won't last forever.

"Nothing is covered up that will not be revealed, or hidden that will not be known" (Lk 12:2). This is a sobering thought. Imagine seeing, face-to-face, the anguish of sin, along with every lost opportunity to love. Who could bear it? Imagine the shame and embarrassment of that moment of honest encounter, especially if it happens after death, when we no longer see dimly but clearly. The burden we feel at that moment will be heavy; it is part of sin's innate punishment.

Yet, even this painful encounter is an act of love from God. As the Church teaches, "Punishments must not be conceived of as a kind of vengeance inflicted by God from without, but as following from the very nature of sin."[17] In other words, God doesn't castigate us; our own sins do. He grants us this mercy even after death, not as punishment, but as a means to be lovingly perfected.

The more I grow in holiness in this life, the easier that day will be. So now is the time to rid ourselves of sinful habits, including one of the most difficult ones — greed.

Some may not be ready to start that journey just yet. I understand the concern: "If I conquer greed, but the other guy doesn't, am I not setting myself up to be used? Won't the greedy always take advantage of the generous?

Matching the other guy's greed with my own is just commonsense self-protection!"

I'm not so naïve as to dismiss the fact that certain individuals get ahead without true cause. There are more than enough examples in daily life. Such has been the case for millennia. Even poor Job wondered, "Why do the wicked live, reach old age, and grow mighty in power?" (Job 21:7).

To this dilemma I would simply say, "Never mind." Greed always collapses of its own deceptive weight. As Psalm 37 reminds us, "Do not fret over him who prospers in his way, over the man who carries out evil devices! Refrain from anger, and forsake wrath! Do not fret; it tends only to evil. For the wicked shall be cut off; but those who wait for the Lord shall possess the land" (Ps 37:7–9).

As the psalm makes clear, it is tempting to respond to evil with anger, to match deception with deception and greed with greed. Scripture wisely counsels patience and fortitude, lest we, too, be drawn into the pit.

This requires great restraint. In these moments it helps to recall a basic teaching in the Catholic Church: grace builds on nature. For years I found this difficult to understand, but it's actually a simple concept. Our path towards holiness begins in our very nature, in the way we were made. Both our gifts and weaknesses present opportunities to grow in holiness. Left to our own devices on the natural level, progress is slow and extremely difficult. "But with God, all things are possible" (Mt 19:26). Grace comes to our aid, helping us perfect what already exists naturally; thus, grace builds on nature.

This mechanism is at work when we strive to overcome greed. Even before we invoke God's help, there is already within us an innate, natural inclination *that rewards generosity, not greed.* It's a simple phenomenon you have likely already experienced. And it's much more powerful than the notion that, for self-preservation, others' greed must be met with your own.

Picture two employers: one is notoriously demanding, shows no appreciation for employees' efforts, and continually tries to stretch the last ounce of production from every worker. The other has rules tempered with leniency for family emergencies, work is expressly appreciated, and employee compensation reflects the fact that success is a team effort. Which company would you want to join? Which company will receive employees' best efforts? Likely, it will be the "generous" company.

Now imagine two employees. One thinks the company owes him a living, gives just enough of his time and energy to get by, and looks for every opportunity to take advantage of the system. The other is thankful that his employer took the financial risk of hiring him, gives an honest day's work, and strives to contribute to the common good. Which employee stands a better chance of promotion? Which will likely be given an opportunity for advancement and greater compensation? Likely, it will be the "generous" employee.

In the long run, whether with employer or employee, generosity begets generosity, and greater success goes to those who have practiced this virtue. There is a sort of natural mechanism beneath the notion that God will provide. Whether you are a boss or a worker, when one develops a generous spirit — when one strives to make it a virtue in his or her life — others can't help but notice. As St. Paul told Timothy: "So also good deeds are conspicuous; and even when they are not, they cannot remain hidden" (1 Tim 5:25).

In other words, the soul shines through. In the long run, more opportunities come to the person who has developed the virtue of generosity. *Others are attracted to this virtue, for we would rather associate with generous people than greedy people.* Thus, the generous soul is more likely to be hired and the generous employer more likely to find loyal employees that help him or her grow even richer. In this way, on a very natural level, God does indeed provide. We might say it's "built into" the way humans interact with each other; and it should give us encouragement when taking our first steps toward the trust that underpins every act of generosity.

The Catholic Church asks three vows of those who wish to enter the religious life: poverty, chastity, and obedience. Why these three? And why are they traditionally listed in just this order? It's as if the Church is saying, "Let's deal with the tough issues right up front: money, sex, and power." Today, these are the areas most likely to be stumbling blocks to holiness, just as they were for those who lived in the time of the Reformation, the Middle Ages, or the early Church: human nature does not change.

The intent behind these public vows is not limited to those who have a vocation as a priest, brother, sister, or a lay member of a secular institute. Rather, poverty, chastity, and obedience are known as the evangelical counsels, and sometimes referred to as the counsels of perfection, because they give guidance to all who wish to strive for perfection in holiness. We, too, can embrace these three counsels in keeping with our own vocation in life. For our purposes at the moment, let's look closer at the counsel of poverty.

To the uninitiated, it may seem odd that poverty is seen by the Church as a good thing, especially when the Church spends so much of her effort to relieve the sufferings caused by poverty. In reality, the vow of poverty simply means detachment from material possessions. It means to live like St. Paul, who told the Philippians, "I have learned, in whatever state I am, to be content. I know how to be abased, and I know how to abound; in any and all circumstances I have learned the secret of facing plenty and hunger, abundance and want" (Phil 4:11–12).

I doubt too many of us have achieved the same attitude, despite what we would like to believe about ourselves. It's easy to look at our possessions and glibly remark, "It's just stuff." But, frankly, how do you know whether you are truly living a life of detachment?

The surest test is to imagine losing everything. Detachment can most clearly be seen when a natural disaster like a flood sweeps through a city. I've done some recovery work, and it amazes me how some people, having lost everything, will say, "It's just stuff," *and mean it.* There is no bitterness in their voice. These are the individuals who truly have attained the counsel of poverty, of detachment from material possessions. They leave the past behind, and seem to psychologically and spiritually recover quite quickly.

Meanwhile, having suffered the same fate, their neighbor grows angry and mourns for months. In their eyes, somebody has to be held responsible for the tragedy, whether local officials for lack of preparedness or God himself for allowing nature to act like nature. Filled with resentment, their interior recovery takes much longer.

So if you wonder whether you are living a life of detachment, imagine yourself losing everything to a natural disaster, and then ask yourself in which camp you would find yourself. It's a difficult mental exercise because it requires great honesty. It's easy to say, "It's just stuff" while we still have our possessions. But if they were lost, could we repeat that phrase without bitterness?

In her wisdom, the Church knows that the sooner we learn detachment, the happier our lives will be. Perhaps that's why the vow of poverty is part of the entrance into consecrated life.

Unfortunately, for the laity, detaching oneself from material possessions is often the last step in our spiritual journey. I've known people, daily communicants recognized for their gentle words and beautiful souls, who could not overcome the final test: money. They could not let go; they could not find the detachment from possessions that would yield the final, missing link in their quest for peace. It's tragic. At an arm's length from perfection, they hold back.

It's been that way for thousands of years. Recall the young man in Matthew's Gospel.

> And behold, one came up to him, saying, "Teacher, what good deed must I do, to have eternal life?" And he said to him, "Why do you ask me about what is good?

One there is who is good. If you would enter life, keep the commandments." He said to him, "Which?" And Jesus said, "You shall not kill, You shall not commit adultery, You shall not steal, You shall not bear false witness, Honor your father and mother, and, You shall love your neighbor as yourself." The young man said to him, "All these I have observed; what do I still lack?" Jesus said to him, "If you would be perfect, go, sell what you possess and give to the poor, and you will have treasure in heaven; and come, follow me." When the young man heard this he went away sorrowful; for he had great possessions. (Mt 19:16–22)

We spoke earlier of striving for perfection. In this light, Jesus' words — "If you would be perfect" — are all the more poignant. Like the young man in this story, dealing with our attachment to possessions is often the last thing we tackle. It was true in Jesus' time, it's true in ours. In my fund-raising work I find many wonderful people living a devout and holy life who, like the young man, mourn at the thought of doing what Jesus asked. Why? Why is this so hard?

Part of the answer lies in the fact that money allows us some modicum of control over our lives; the less we have, the more dependent we become on the Lord. To give away money is to replace control of my future with trust that God will provide. That's a scary thought.

It's one thing for me to pray, "Jesus, I trust in you" while I'm comfortable and well fed. My prayer would take on a whole new meaning if I were hungry and about to lose my home.

But there is another reason that detachment and generosity are often the final virtues to be attained, and greed the last vice we conquer. The answer rests in our nature.

Many vices are more difficult to indulge as we get older. Take, for example, gluttony or lust. These are, to some extent, self-correcting vices. At some point the glutton develops diabetes, heart ailments, or a host of other problems; nature itself forces a change in behavior. The same is true of lust. As humans age, desires naturally wane. It becomes easier to live a chaste life in both thought and action.

Not so with greed. As we get older, most people tend to have more money, so the magnetic attraction of what we've accumulated draws us ever stronger. Unlike gluttony and lust, which become *easier* to confront as we mature — thanks to the natural mechanisms of the aging body — greed becomes *more* difficult. In this sense, greed is a unique vice. Age actually works against us. The more we have, the more we want. And the more we want, the more we become attached to our possessions in a never-ending cycle. *This is why enough is never enough.*

The only way to break the cycle is to turn toward those things that last.

All people desire to leave a lasting mark.
But what endures? Money does not.
Even buildings do not, nor books. After
a certain time, longer or shorter, all these

things disappear. The only thing that lasts for ever is the human soul, the human person created by God for eternity.

The fruit that endures is therefore all that we have sown in human souls: love, knowledge, a gesture capable of touching hearts, words that open the soul to joy in the Lord. So let us go and pray to the Lord to help us bear fruit that endures. Only in this way will the earth be changed from a valley of tears to a garden of God.[18]

FOR REFLECTION

Everything you own you will one day give away. Everything.

1. What plans have you made to glorify God? After you die, what would you like to do with your assets to leave a lasting mark? Have some fun. Be creative.

2. Share your ideas with your money partner.

Endnotes

1. Michael Shermer, *The Mind of the Market: How Biology and Psychology Shape Our Economic Lives* (New York: Holt Paperbacks, 2008), pp. 145–146.

2. Richard Easterlin, "Diminishing Marginal Utility of Income? Caveat Emptor," *Social Indicators Research* 70, no. 3 (2005): 249.

3. This experience has some backing in research. Richard Easterlin asks, "Does more money make people happier? To judge from survey responses, most people certainly think so, although there is a limit. When asked how much more money they would need to be completely happy, people typically name a figure greater than their current income by about 20 percent. At all levels of income, the typical response is that one needs 20% more to be happy." Richard A. Easterlin, "The Economics of Happiness," *Daedalus* 133, no. 2 (2004): 26–33.

4. In using the traditional term "Man," I do not wish to offend anyone's sensibilities. At the same time, there is no single word or phrase that adequately conveys all that "Man" implies. The term is employed intentionally as the only word capable of conveying "Man" in the fullest sense as male and female, *as an individual and corporate identity,* as the first man Adam and as the last man Jesus Christ (cf. Gn 1:26–27, 1 Cor 15:45–49).

    To substitute "human being" is to limit our concept of the person to the language of physical science; we are a species of animal. Likewise, "humanity" is the language of philosophy and sociology, referring to the entire collection of human beings, nothing more. In short, language sets the parameters for what we can and cannot discuss. To allow the word "Man" to slip into disuse is to leave the realm of theology and limit oneself to words better suited for science, philosophy, and sociology.

5. Ibid. Shermer, p. 148.

6. Gerald Prante, "Summary of Latest Federal Individual Income Tax Data," *Fiscal Facts,* Fiscal Fact No. 183, July 30, 2009,

http://www.taxfoundation.org/publications/show/250.html. Accessed 11/12/09.

7. "Shoplifters and Dishonest Employees Are Apprehended in Record Numbers by US Retailers," http://www.hayesinternational.com/thft_srvys.html. Accessed 11/12/09. The annual survey is conducted by Jack L. Hayes International, Inc., a loss-prevention consulting firm. Their 21st Annual Retail Theft Survey included twenty-two major retailers.

8. Ibid.

9. The Order of Mass, Communion Rite.

10. *Catechism of the Catholic Church*, Second Edition, United States Catholic Conference, Inc., Washington, DC, 1997. Paragraph 2725.

11. *Webster's Revised Unabridged Dictionary*, 1913 Edition, p. 628. Accessed online at: http://machaut.uchicago.edu/?action=search&word=glamour&resource=Webster%27s&quicksearch=on.

12. *Rite of Christian Initiation of Adults*, Liturgy Training Publications, Chicago,1988, par. 224, p. 140.

13. CCC 2733.

14. CCC 2094.

15. Cf. Nicholas D. Kristof, "Bleeding Heart Tightwads," *The New York Times*, 12/20/08. In an op-ed piece, Mr. Kristof writes, "Liberals show tremendous compassion in pushing for generous government spending to help the neediest people at home and abroad. Yet when it comes to individual contributions to charitable causes, liberals are cheapskates.

"Arthur Brooks, the author of a book on donors to charity — *Who Really Cares* — cites data that households headed by conservatives give 30 percent more to charity than households headed by liberals. A study by Google found an even greater disproportion: average annual contributions reported by conservatives were almost double those of liberals.

"Other research has reached similar conclusions. The 'generosity index' from the *Catalogue for Philanthropy* typically finds that red states are the most likely to give to nonprofits, while Northeastern states are least likely to do so.

"The upshot is that Democrats, who speak passionately about the hungry and homeless, personally fork over less money to charity than Republicans: the ones who try to cut health insurance for children.

"'When I started doing research on charity,' Mr. Brooks wrote, 'I expected to find that political liberals — who, I believed, genuinely cared more about others than conservatives did — would turn out to be the most privately charitable people. So when my early findings led me to the opposite conclusion, I assumed I had made some sort of technical error. I re-ran analyses. I got new data. Nothing worked. In the end, I had no option but to change my views.'"

16. Lawrence Mishel, Jared Bernstein, and Heidi Shierholz, "The State of Working America 2008/2009," p. 220, policy paper presented by the Economic Policy Institute, http://www.stateofworkingamerica .org/swa08-exec_pay.pdf. Accessed 11/27/09.

17. See the *Catechism of the Catholic Church*, paragraph 1472.

18. Homily of His Eminence Cardinal Joseph Ratzinger, Dean of the College of Cardinals, Vatican Basilica, Monday, 18 April 2005. From: http://www.vatican.va/gpII/documents/homily-pro-eligendo-pontifice_20050418_en.html. Accessed 11-19-09.